A TRANSFORMING VISION
Suffering and Glory in God's World

Cape Town 1993

THE OFFICIAL REPORT OF THE JOINT MEETING OF THE PRIMATES OF THE ANGLICAN COMMUNION AND THE ANGLICAN CONSULTATIVE COUNCIL

Story: John Martin
Editors: Laura McGeary and James Rosenthal

Published for the Anglican Communion
by Church House Publishing

Acknowledgements

The official documentation of the Joint Meeting of the Primates of the Anglican Communion and the Anglican Consultative Council, January 1993, University of the Western Cape.
Hosted by the Church of the Province of Southern Africa

The Most Revd and Rt Hon. George L. Carey, President
The Revd Canon Colin Craston, Chairman
The Rt Revd Simon Chiwanga, Vice Chairman
The Revd Canon Samuel Van Culin, Secretary General

Those who made this report possible:

John Martin, Writer
James Rosenthal, Director of Communications
Laura McGeary, Editor
Staff writers: James Thrall, Paul Richardson, Patrick Forbes, Gordon Light, Pat Mauney, Liz Gibson Harries, Doug Tindal, Charles Long, John Allen
Anglican Communion News Service Photographs: Lynn Ross, Patrick Forbes, James Rosenthal, Stewart Ting Chong, James Thrall
Artists: Giles Harcourt, Bob Comin
CHP: Bill Burford and Robin Brookes
Secretariat Co-ordinator: Christine Codner
Special thanks to: Elizabeth Coy, Deirdre Martin and the Revd Canon Roger Symon

---

ISBN 0 7151 4829 X

Published 1993 for the Anglican Communion Office,
Partnership House, 157 Waterloo Road, London SE1 8UT
by Church House Publishing,
Church House, Great Smith Street, London SW1P 3NZ

© The Secretary General of the Anglican Consultative Council 1993

All rights reserved. No part of this publication may be reproduced in any form or by any means, electronic or mechanical, including photo-copying, recording, or any information storage and retrieval system, without permission in writing from the copyright owner.

Printed by Rapier Press Ltd

Foreword

by
The Archbishop of Canterbury

The theme of the January 1993 meeting of the Primates of the Anglican Communion and the Anglican Consultative Council was 'A Transforming Vision – Suffering and Glory in God's World'.

We met in Cape Town as guests of the Church of the Province of Southern Africa. The Archbishop and Metropolitan, the Most Revd Desmond Mpilo Tutu, shared the warmth and vitality of this strong Church, and invited us to meet church and political leaders who helped us see the effects of apartheid on the people of this wonderful land.

The sights, sounds and experiences of South Africa overwhelmed us, and constantly lifted our spirits. Arriving in Cape Town, we came with the prayers and concerns of our respective Provinces. As the days progressed, however, we realised that our theme was particularly appropriate to South Africa, and those whose struggle has been aided by a strong faith in the power of the resurrection.

Throughout the visit, in country parish and township, at the Day of Celebration in the Good Hope Centre and at St George's Cathedral, I felt proud of our people, young and old alike, of all races, in the Church of the Province of Southern Africa.

I commend to you the story of our meeting and the photographs and documents contained in this volume. As people with a memory, a message, and a mission we were able to share our worship, deliberations and experiences together in an atmosphere abounding in Christ's love. We came away with our vision of Christ renewed, and of his power to transform human life.

For such an experience, one that will be cherished for years to come, we say thanks be to God.

God bless Africa!

+ George Cantuar

A plenary session in Cape Town

Introduction

The last decade in my life has brought me in touch with people from around the world in a most intimate way. Meeting after meeting and visit after visit, the realisation that the Anglican Communion is home to people of over 160 countries and a multitude of languages makes me feel glad to be part of this family.

Each meeting of the Primates and the ACC has had its unique place at a particular moment in time, the Church finding itself as an instrument of peace and love in an often divided and sad world.

The Lambeth Conference 1988, of which I had the privilege of serving as secretary, was another milestone in the Church's coming to grips with the fact that its diversity was one of its richest gifts. The presence of translators, various people in national dress, as well as different forms of worship, pointed to a Church, led by the Spirit, that responds to the call of God's people in their need.

The first ever joint meeting of the Primates and the ACC, the story of which follows here alongside resolutions, the Archbishop of Canterbury's sermons, and the plenary presentations, has come at yet another time of transition for the Church and for me personally as I prepare to retire.

As we gathered at the University of the Western Cape, January 1993, we saw the beauty of the land, the people and weather. We affirmed the courageous witness of the Church of the Province of Southern Africa, being hosted by the compelling person of Archbishop Desmond, and under the confident leadership of Archbishop George. There were the experiences and encounters that made me sad – those that made me glad – all combining to allow me to end my term as Secretary-General knowing full well that out of political, ecclesial and personal struggle and suffering can come glory. One could see the expectation and hope of glory on the faces of the people of Southern Africa and could actually feel it in the warmth of their touch and the graciousness of their hospitality.

How is it possible? Their pains of inequality, the lack of the most basic human rights, the apartheid that has yet to die – all still exist in South Africa, we saw it before our very eyes. How is it possible? The concerns that plague us as a Church – where does one group fit in the Communion as opposed to another? Where will we get the money to increase programmes rather than fall back in shyness and failure? How is it possible? The provinces shared in the personal traumas of people in their churches

Introduction

victimised by war, hatred, poverty, natural disaster, family strife, fear, homelessness, disease. How is it possible that we sing and pray and move forward in faith?

The answer lies in what we as Anglicans believe about God. The fact that God took flesh to share in our suffering. Through faith in Jesus Christ, the word-made-flesh, a transforming vision of changing suffering to glory can be our experience. It is God's gift to those who believe.

Is such a belief possible? Again our meeting in Cape Town points to a simple fact that the faithful of this province of our Communion continue to face the trauma of suffering as well as the fear of the unknown, for who is to predict the road that must be travelled to a democracy in a non-racial state, with a vision – Proverbs warns that without vision the people die.

Thus rooted in the historic catholic tradition of Anglicanism, matured in the suffering and afflictions of living in an unjust society, the Church in Southern Africa lives a committed, lively and involved Christian witness that was visualised dramatically on 24 January at the Good Hope Centre with over 10,000 present at the Holy Eucharist with Archbishop Desmond and Archbishop George. Our fellowship of prayer was dramatically centred at the altar by the presence of representatives of the entire Communion gathered at the great celebration of our redemption, the vision of the eternal banquet which we all will share in God's time. As one of the dozens of priests administering Holy Communion, I was touched and inspired by the simplicity and honesty of spirit that surrounded me in the vast arena.

The Church in Southern Africa has a vision, and I believe the Communion, as represented by the leaders meeting in Cape Town, also has a vision. What is that vision? – the Church of Uganda with its AIDS education scheme, the meeting's concern over the Palestinian deportees in the Middle East, speaking to sex abuse, eagerness to maintain an openness for people within the church whose views differ on theological and doctrinal issues and rejoicing with the growth of the Church most notably in Rwanda, Zaire, and Burundi and the forthcoming inauguration of the Province of Korea – the strength of the Episcopal Church of the Sudan, also vexed with living in a country beset with violence, perplexed by fear and mistrust. These all witness to a people with hope and vision.

Indeed the vision must be of a church, alive and working to bring God's kingdom to fulfilment. A church open and accepting, a church with a message that can transform our pain and sorrow into joy and give purpose to lives seeking to serve the Christ they encounter in others on this pilgrimage of life. The Presiding Bishop of the Episcopal Church USA, the Most Revd Edmond Browning, has been consistent in his insistence that the Church be a place where there are 'no outcasts' – but where all can come and be transformed.

Introduction

I thank God for giving me ten years of service as Secretary General. I thank God for the people from all over the Communion that have helped me in our mutual work towards the fulfilment of the vision that is ours as Christ's body here on earth. I thank God for those in the ecumenical church that share our vision and labour with us for the advancement of the kingdom.

The one-time Dean of Westminster, Eric Symes Abbott, in his book *Invitation to Prayer* says, 'There is no dichotomy between prayer and action. Prayer is the time God uses to love and reincarnate himself in us, and activity is the normal expression of this love. God loves in us, and others through us.'

Those gathered in Cape Town felt and saw this prayer and action come to life. May this be our vision as Anglicans as the struggles continue and the glory is revealed more and more for each of us in the days and years ahead.

The Revd Canon Samuel Van Culin
London
The Presentation of Our Lord, 2 February 1993

Opening press statement by Archbishop Carey at Cape Town Lahan Airport

It is a great moment for me today to set foot on African soil for the first time. In the 21 months since I became Archbishop of Canterbury, I have travelled to the South Pacific, the United States, Asia and the Middle East; but this is the first time my wife and I have come to Africa. I have heard so much about this beautiful land of yours and its people are so closely linked by history to England and I am delighted to be here at last.

The Churches of the Anglican Communion have many strong ties and shared traditions. I have always felt a special honour and affection for our Church here. It is therefore the greatest pleasure to be welcomed by my friend and fellow Archbishop, Desmond Tutu, and his wife Leah, and by Anglican friends from the Church of the Province. I am also very pleased to be welcomed by Councillor Keegan, representing the Mayor of Cape Town and the Mayor of Bellville where we are to stay at the University of the Western Cape.

As you know, I am here to attend the first joint meeting of the Primates of the Anglican Communion and the Anglican Consultative Council. We represent a world-wide Communion of Churches and we belong to every continent and culture. We have come to consult with each other about a whole range of subjects that concern the way we witness to Christ in the contemporary world.

I believe the Church today has a critical role to play in the world as an international community of peace and justice committed to the way of Jesus Christ.

All over the world – in Europe (and not least in my own country), in the Middle East, in Africa, in Asia – political conflict is entangled with religious belief; and all over the world poverty and inequality fuel violence and unrest. Christianity can of course be distorted to serve selfish ends, but it remains a powerful force for good and harmony. I believe that the Church in Southern Africa has been a wonderful example of the ministry of prophecy and reconciliation to which Christ calls us, and Anglicans all over the world are proud of its fine achievements.

I am thrilled about the end of the civil war in Mozambique and the inde-

Opening press statement

pendence of Namibia but deeply concerned about the renewed outbreaks of fighting in Angola, where the Province of Southern Africa has pastoral responsibilities.

The world is waiting impatiently for South Africa to introduce a new dispensation soon. Anglicans throughout the world, who have consistently prayed for a resolution of your problems, want to see an end to the distressing violence which prevails in so many parts of your country. We should also like to see a multi-party democracy in which there is tolerance of opposing viewpoints and free political activity for all. We pray that the cries of ordinary South Africans for a new era of security and prosperity will be answered soon.

I look forward to meeting South Africans and to conversations with the State President, Mr Mandela, Dr Buthelezi and other political leaders, and to catch something of the character of this great nation.

We are delighted therefore to be here as your guests during the next two weeks. Our whole conference will pray that constitutional progress will be swift and peaceful, so that all South Africans may look forward confidently to the day when they can live together in peace and stability.

CAPE TOWN AIRPORT
16 January 1993

Arriving at Cape Town airport

'I have a dream of a renewed Anglicanism, reaching out in service, in glad obedience to the Lord of the Church, contemptuous of survival but expectant that the Christ who calls us to go into the world will keep us until his Kingdom comes.' *Archbishop George Carey.*

A Pastoral Letter

We greet you from Cape Town, at the end of the first joint meeting of the Primates of the Anglican Communion and the Anglican Consultative Council. Grace and peace to you from God, the source and sustainer of all life, who redeems, sanctifies, and calls us to be witnesses to his immeasurable love in Christ.

Our theme has been 'A Transforming Vision – Suffering and Glory in God's World'. We were privileged to see at first hand something of the work and witness of our hosts, the Church of the Province of Southern Africa. We listened to stories from the Anglican family throughout the world, sharing in one another's joys and pain. We were encouraged and energised to learn how often through suffering the Church in so many places is being renewed and the glory of God is being revealed.

1. A VISION

'Where there is no vision, the people perish' (Prov. 29.18). Our fundamental need is for a vision of God. As creator: we are totally dependent on him for our life. As redeemer: through the suffering and resurrection of Christ we have a living hope which can sustain us whatever our circumstances. As life giving power: we have more than human resources available to us in our daily work and witness.

This vision has practical implications for us as individuals and as Churches. It is:

- a vision for the renewal of evangelism in the Anglican Communion, with bishops, clergy and laity taking the initiative to share the Good News of Jesus Christ, a vision of a transformed and revitalised local church, where every member has a part as an active agent in God's mission;
- a vision of the Good News bringing unity to the divided, and dignity to the poor;
- a vision of all faiths listening to one another and respecting one another;
- a vision of men and women working together in partnership and freedom, responding to God's call to reflect his image; with young people well grounded in the life of faith and offering their gifts of energy and creativity.

Archbishop Carey at the scene of the bombing in Warrington, England

2. SUFFERING AND GLORY

We are grateful to God for many new signs of hope around the world: the moves towards a democratic and non-racial society in South Africa; the prospect of lasting peace in Mozambique, Somalia, the Philippines and El Salvador; progress towards multi-party democracy in many countries of Africa; the end of the Cold War and decline of the threat of nuclear war; changes in Eastern Europe, which present new opportunities to spread the Good News.

Yet as we come towards the middle of the last decade of the twentieth century, we are faced with many sober realities which challenge our Churches: oppression and violence in the world in the name of religion and nationalism, and the spectre of ethnic cleansing; the threat of a marketplace which can ignore the needs of the poor and weak; the re-emergence of racism in an increasingly insular Western Europe; loss of faith and the sense of meaning in so many societies and cultures; the rampant spread of the scourge of AIDS; the burden of personal and national debt, and its crippling effect on the countries of the Third World; the threat of global ecological disaster caused by human greed; cheapening of human life through seemingly unending conflicts in Liberia, the Sudan, Angola, Northern Ireland, the Arabian Gulf, and the unresolved Israeli-Palestinian conflict; continuing violence in South Africa.

Twenty-seven centuries ago Isaiah the prophet was overcome by the spectre of despair, and cried 'O Lord, how long?'. In many different parts of the world God's people are uttering this same cry. Through the prophet God revealed that amid all the suffering and turmoil, he was working out his purposes and making his glory known.

We are therefore called to be a people of hope:

- to be partners with God in the renewal of the whole of creation;
- working for peace, justice and reconciliation, in our families, our communities, and in the international family of nations;
- promoting human rights, and working for the transformation of our communities;
- giving generously of our time and our resources to people in need;
- sustaining our commitment to Christian unity, especially by upholding the authority of episcopal jurisdiction in our dioceses, being determined to offer pastoral care to all, recognising the integrity both of those who cannot accept women priests and those who can.

A Pastoral Letter

3. ACTION

We have been entrusted with A Transforming Vision. To realise this vision, we call on all the Churches of the Anglican Communion to commit themselves to:

- a life of sustained prayer which intercedes for the whole world family in their joys and hurts, and the communities from which we come;
- inviting neighbours, friends and colleagues to join them in the fellowship of worship, making their churches places of welcome and friendship;
- opening their homes, to offer hospitality and refuge, and so to share the love of God revealed in Jesus.
- equipping the people of God with a confidence in the Gospel to transform their everyday lives.

May God bless you in his service.

+ George Cantuar, President of the Anglican Consultative Council
and *Primus inter pares*
Canon Colin Craston, Chairman of the Anglican Consultative Council

'One of the problems with the Church today is that we're so busy singing our liturgy that we're deaf to the songs of celebration and sadness going on around us.' *Archbishop George Carey.*

The Story

The Story
John Martin

Those of us who had the privilege of sharing in the joint meeting of the Primates of the Anglican Communion and the Anglican Consultative Council in Cape Town, January 1993, came away with indelible memories. There will be memories of the people we met, or with whom we renewed friendships. The sheer variety of the people who came to Cape Town as representatives of their Churches and the stories they told of God at work, left us with renewed confidence in our calling to serve Christ wherever we are.

There will be special memories of our hosts, the Church of the Province of Southern Africa. We had a taste of their worship, both at the massive Eucharist at Cape Town's Good Hope Centre, and in parish churches in which we were guests. We heard something of the witness and the suffering of a Church which has been constantly in our prayers for decades. We listened to the vision of the future shared by some of their political leaders. All that will prompt us to pray even more fervently for the future course of this beautiful country.

As to the meeting itself, questions emerged which will ring in our ears for some time to come. There was plenty of evidence to suggest the importance of the Canterbury connection, those bonds of affection which hold together a Communion of 80 million possessed of a huge variety of cultures and traditions. Hard questions were raised about both the cost and the effectiveness of the various Anglican instruments of consultation – the Lambeth Conference, the Primates' Meeting and the Anglican Consultative Council. What is their specific purpose, how are they to relate to one another, and are there other possible models for serving a world-wide Communion which is episcopally-led and synodically governed?

Many of these questions were focused by the Archbishop of Canterbury in an address to the Primates at the beginning of their day in retreat. In an exposition of Phil. 2, he touched the core of the Christian understanding of spiritual leadership: our Lord's distrust of power and his determination to empty himself to enter into the life of humanity as a slave. These matters will be the core of the agenda of the next Inter-Anglican Theological and Doctrinal Commission.

The Story

The joint meeting of the Primates of the Anglican Communion and the Anglican Consultative Council was in effect an experiment. So too is this report. Unlike previous Reports of the ACC, which were drafted by the various Section Groups, the story of the meeting is essentially the work of a single author. Official documentation follows.

One of my main priorities as writer/editor has been to bring the reader a cross section of the stories shared by delegates who came to Cape Town. In this Decade of Evangelism we have two stories to share: the story of Jesus Christ and our own story. I hope what follows will inspire us with a fresh vision to share them both.

✢

A Vision that Transforms

As with the 1988 Lambeth Conference, delegates appreciated the Bible studies held at the start of each day. Unlike Lambeth, studies were not assigned to a single leader. Instead, each day, a different speaker introduced a passage from John's Gospel and then invited delegates gathered round tables to spend half an hour discussing questions on the text.

The Archbishop of Canterbury led the first and the final study. In his first presentation he said that John's Gospel 'takes us to the heart of the vision where suffering and glory jostle side by side'. If we follow Christ, he said, we must be ready to face rejection.

The point was immediately illustrated by the second study. It was to have been led by the Archbishop of Nigeria but had to be read by Bishop Maxwell Anikwenwa. The Archbishop's passport had been withdrawn after he sent an outspoken letter to the President about the situation in the country. In Archbishop Adetiloye's address he spoke of 'rioting Muslim fanatics who force Christians to recite the Muslim password Allah Akbar! on pain of brutal death, maiming or the loss of property and employment'.

The Bible studies were an opportunity for delegates to tell their own stories and share insights. One oft-repeated remark was from Bishop Mark Dyer who said in the fourth study that we can only see God in Jesus, 'through the smoked glass of humanity and not otherwise'. He took up the vivid image of Christ the Good Shepherd who fulfilled Isaiah's prophecy of the one who would be 'so much one of the flock that he would become the lamb slain for the people'.

The joint meeting opened with a retreat conducted by Canon Francis Cull, who gave separate addresses to the Primates and ACC and preached at a Eucharist. Canon Cull, who is 78, heads an Institute for Spirituality in

Cape Town, providing spiritual direction and workshops on prayer for clergy and laity.

A Vision of God

EXTRACTS FROM TALKS GIVEN BY CANON FRANCIS CULL

At a great time of crisis in Old Testament history, the Book of Samuel records, 'The word of the Lord was very rare'. There was no vision. And in Prov. 29.18 we read: 'Where there is no vision, the people perish.' Both speak of a deafness to God's voice, a deafness to his word, a spirit of apostasy. So what do we need to achieve that transforming vision?

1. A vision of God as creator
We are more than dependent on God, we are contingent. Let me explain that word by analogy. When the child is in the womb it is contingent upon the mother. It can't live without the mother. But when the child is born, when it's at the breast, it is dependent on her. We are never just dependent on God. We are always contingent.

'If I make my bed in hell, thou art there . . . if I take the wings of the morning and fly to the uttermost parts of the earth, even there thy hand will guide me.'

2. A vision of God as redeemer
There was a boy who was clever with his hands. He made himself a boat. He fixed a mast and a sail and went down to the sea to sail it. One day an extra big wave came along. He couldn't swim well, and he saw his boat disappearing out to sea. He was very sad, because he had made his boat. And if you have made a boat it is very precious.

A few weeks later he was walking by some shops and he saw his boat in a window. He knew it was his, because once you have made something you know it. He went in and he said to the man, 'Excuse me, but that boat in the window is mine.'

Now the man thought, 'This seems an honest boy.' So he said he would sell it for what it had cost him, two rand. The boy went home and found he had just 20 cents. He got another 20 cents from his uncle. He went inside and found his sister there with her boyfriend, and said to him: 'Give me a rand, and I'll go away.'

Finally he got the money together and went back to get the boat. And as the boy was going out he was hugging his boat, talking to his boat. He said:

The Story

'You are mine. You are twice mine. I made you, and I bought you.' That is the meaning of the Cross. God says, 'You are twice mine. I made you. And when you had gone away on the rough sea of sin and self, I bought you by the Cross.'

3. A vision of God as spiritual dynamic
We perhaps sometimes forget that we belong to a society which is meant to be revolutionary. When the Apostles were brought before the magistrates the charge was: 'These men having turned the world upside down have come hither.' This is precisely what the world needs: to be turned upside-down.

Every revolution needs a leader, a programme, a dynamic. We have a leader, Jesus. We have a programme, expressed in many ways, coming back to Jesus. We have a dynamic, a living Christ, through whom we become, and are becoming, a new person. 'For if any be in Christ there is a new creation.'

A few years ago a young Salvation Army officer was very distressed because the Salvation Army seemed to have lost its evangelistic thrust. And he decided he would go to the tomb of General William Booth. So he made a pilgrimage and went and knelt at the tomb. There was the General's name and that great Salvation Army phrase, 'Promoted to Glory'. He prayed the prayer which the General prayed over all those lost people of the great cities of England and Europe. Then he prayed this prayer: 'Do it again, Lord, do it again.' That is all.

In us, revive your Church, Lord. Begin with me.

A Vision for Ourselves

In his second talk Fr Cull took the three letters 'ACC' and used them to suggest some things that are vital to personal spiritual health and to the spiritual health of the entire Church.

'A' stands for affirming God's love for us. God loves me unconditionally, warts and all. I said to one of my children: 'Does God love you most when you're good or when you're bad?' 'Er,' he said, 'when I'm good!' I said, 'No!' 'When I'm bad then?' 'No.' 'What then?' 'Always.'

'A' stands for the acceptance of our giftedness. God does not make garbage or junk. God makes people in his own image, very beautiful. And if any of you doubt that, I would beg of you to go and look in the mirror and say to yourself and God, I am very beautiful. And the greatest gift we have is the gift of ourselves. God gave us life, and he gave it to us to use for his

A Vision for Ourselves

glory. And we're very gifted. I know we have to recognise the poverty of our response to God. But let us start always by recognising our giftedness.

'A' stands for adoration. The Church, in its worship, constantly calls us, in the Eucharist and amidst morning and evening prayer, to offer adoration to God. There was a French peasant named Pierre. Every evening as he came back from the fields he would slip into the church. When he went into the local bistro to have a drink with his friends, they would laugh at him and say, 'Pierre, why do you go there? You're not one of these holy nuns or a priest. Yet you do that every day. What do you say?' And he said: 'I don't say anything. He looks at me and I look at him, and we're both happy.'

'C' stands for confession. I need to learn to confess my sinfulness. I'm convinced that there is only one sin. And that sin is my refusal to respond to God's love. That sin make take many forms. It may take the form of gluttony and drunkenness and the misuse of my sexual powers. It may be envy, hatred or malice of envy, condoning of structural sin. Each one of those sins is just a part of saying 'I reject your love.' Religion is the living 'yes' to God. Sin is very monotonous. If anyone can come up with a new sin they'll have really made my day.

'C' stands for confirming my desire to be truly penitent and to come to the Cross. If we're going to have renewal in the Church, if the Decade of Evangelism is going to mean anything, it will be because individuals in the Church discover, or rediscover, the person of Jesus.

> Christ for me . . . on the Cross.
> Christ before me . . . my example.
> Christ in me . . . the living power.
>
> Christ for me . . . my Saviour.
> Christ before me . . . my example.
> Christ in me . . . my dynamic.

'C' stands for the need to consecrate myself. Jesus said: 'For their sakes I consecrate myself.' In another translation: 'For their sakes I sanctify myself.' 'Sanctify' means that which I am going to do personally to make me holy, in order that people who see holiness in me may think better of our Father in heaven. Consecrate means to offer, personally to offer something and never want it back. When the sacrifice was placed on the altar nothing was to come back. It was to be burnt wholly. So when Jesus said 'I consecrate myself' he knew he was going to the Cross and that only his death, his total offering, was of any value.

The last 'C' is contemplation. There are two main evils that the Church

The Story

suffers from, especially in this age. The first evil is pietism. It's that evil that makes the Church a holy huddle, the club mentality. People gather in the Church. They don't want to grow. They don't want to change, or rock the boat. Then there is the other type, where vast crowds turn up. It's what I call the pub mentality. Now if you go into a pub, they won't ask you if the woman you are with is your wife. All they're interested in is that you buy more and more to drink. The other evil the Church suffers is the lowering of the standards. Pietism on the one hand. Multitudinism on the other. And that leads to an activism which ultimately leads to the glory of the men and women who belong to it, and never the glory of God. There is no more wonderful way of interceding than to contemplate God, and just be with him in adoration and stillness, lost in wonder, love and praise.

Canon Francis Cull is director of the Institute for Spirituality, Church of the Province of Southern Africa.

'Silence is the language of God. Everything else is a bad translation.'

Bishop Mark Dyer, USA.

+

The Southern African context

THE CONTRASTS OF CAPE TOWN

When Sir Francis Drake rounded the Cape in 1577 he described it as 'the fairest Cape that I have seen in the whole circumference of the Earth.' Once known as the Cape of Storms, the Cape was renamed the Cape of Good Hope as early explorers and merchants looked across the Indian Ocean to the treasures of the Indian Sub-Continent.

Cape Town is a busy seaport astride the Atlantic and Indian Oceans. It is also a thriving commercial and tourist centre. Its two universities, Cape Town and the Western Cape, provide a rich variety of opportunities for higher education.

Tourist guides, with their rapturous prose extolling the fine restaurants and hotels, the splendour of Table Mountain, the white sandy beaches, give no hint of what may be found on the fringes of this city, the townships, the squatter camps with their shacks built from other people's refuse on sand in which no flowers or vegetables can grow. Nothing prepares the visitor for the shock of seeing thousands and thousands of people living in such conditions. One is drawn in immediately by the warm welcome and the dignity of the people.

Cape Town, like many cities, is a city of stark contrasts, immense wealth and horrendous poverty. It is, nonetheless, a city of hope, good hope. It is a city where a start is being made on co-operatively planned new housing areas, like Blue Downs where the development officer is a priest.

And Cape Town, for all its wealth and with all its poverty is the city that made the ACC/Primates welcome in 1993.

10,000 TURN OUT FOR CAPE EUCHARIST

Cape Town diocese gave the Archbishop of Canterbury and the Joint Meeting a rousing welcome. Not a seat was left in the Good Hope Centre. People stood in the gangways to form the largest congregation Archbishop George Carey had ever addressed. Archbishop Desmond Tutu presided at a service lasting almost three hours.

Archbishop Carey called for a new vision for Africa. 'Few people can be unmoved by the terrible suffering that afflicts the great continent of Africa. Africa lies wounded and bleeding, and we who live elsewhere must not pass by on the other side. No Christian can be excused from coming to the aid of our African brothers and sisters in need.'

He went on to make a special reference to South Africa. 'Today we meet in a country where the scourge of apartheid has left deep scars of violence, shame and anger on black and white alike. In these last decades, families have been destroyed, homes demolished and whole neighbourhoods dumped in alien land; innocent people have been detained and abused by inhuman treatment; a whole population has been subjugated by an evil system.'

On the recent changes in South Africa, Archbishop Carey said, 'It is right to be grateful for the promise of freedom: it is wrong to neglect the appalling pain and agony that you have suffered. Christ has been recrucified again and again in South Africa.'

The Diocese was present in full force and colour. The Mothers' Union, the Girls' and Boys' Brigade were highly visible, alongside hundreds of acolytes and servers and 60 ministers assisting with distribution of Communion. A massed choir drawn from Cape Town parishes supplied a rich musical setting for a traditional yet lively Anglican rite, reflecting the predominant Anglo-Catholic tradition of the Diocese, complete with incense, banners and colourful African vestments. A troupe of liturgical dancers played a part, together with a brass band. Music ranged across

The Procession at the Good Hope Centre

The Southern African context

The Secretary General is one of 60 ministers of Holy Communion during the Day of Celebration Eucharist

every possible tradition from indigenous African tunes, the hymns of Charles Wesley and John Newton, to Anglican chant.

Afterwards delegates adjourned to the Cape Town Civic Centre for a lunch hosted by the Deputy Mayor, Councillor Clive Keegan.

PROGRESS IN SOUTH AFRICA

Members of the joint meeting said they were 'shocked' that the lives of ordinary South Africans had shown little improvement 'despite three years of talks about democracy'. In a resolution which welcomed Namibia's independence, peace in Mozambique, and news of planned elections in Lesotho, the joint conference also called for free political activity and democracy in Swaziland.

'In South Africa we thank God for the movement, however slow and halting, towards a non-racial democracy.' the resolution said. It paid tribute to 'the millions of South Africans who sacrificed so much to bring pressure on the minority government to change its course'.

The conference acknowledged the courage of President F.W. de Klerk for initiating changes in February 1990. But it also said it shared with many South Africans 'their frustration at the slow pace of constitutional talks', and identified with them in condemning 'the failure of the [South African] government to act vigorously to end the violence which wracks the country'. 'We are shocked,' the resolution added, 'that despite three years of talks about democracy there is scant evidence of any meaningful improvements in the lives of ordinary South Africans.' During visits to black townships in Cape Town earlier in the week, members of the joint conference were struck by the poverty they saw.

Archbishop Keith Rayner of Australia urged the conference to drop a sentence in the resolution which called on South Africa's political leaders 'not to play with the lives of people by tactics of clinging to power, of point-scoring, of grandstanding and brinkmanship'. It was an undiplomatic and inappropriate statement for this body to make, he said. Archbishop Desmond Tutu thanked Archbishop Rayner for 'speaking pastorally and caringly', but said that such a statement was 'quite crucial for our people'.

'There are many of our leaders who have been playing ducks and drakes with our people,' he said. 'We are not all outsiders; we [South Africans] are here too. We are a family. It will not be taken amiss,' he said.

The resolution also called for:

- the speedy introduction of interim arrangements for multi-party rule pending elections;
- elections during 1993;
- an end to whites-only military conscription.

On sanctions, the conference said the international community should be guided by representatives of the victims of apartheid, and said it stood by Archbishop Tutu's call that sanctions be lifted only when the government acted to end violence or there was multiparty control of the security forces.

The joint meeting applauded Anglican leaders for 'putting all political leaders and parties under the scrutiny to which the government was subjected in the days when many other parties were outlawed', and pledged its support to South African churches when it spoke for the weak and against those who misused power.

MEMBERS HEAR POLITICAL LEADERS

The joint meeting was an opportunity to meet and hear South Africa's three main political leaders. The Archbishop of Canterbury and other leaders had an hour-long meeting with the South African President. Mr F.W. de Klerk

The Southern African context

The visit of Nelson Mandela

described it as 'very constructive, very warm, very friendly'.

The Anglican Communion delegation pledged their support to help bring about democratic change in South Africa. According to Mr de Klerk, much of the discussion focused on the country's 'economic problems and the plight of South Africans as a result'. It also explored 'solutions and the hopes that we have for 1993'. The State President said the international Christian community had already made a great contribution to the South African government's move away from apartheid, but 'at some times some of the more aggressive actions delayed change'.

Asked about the economic sanctions still partially imposed against South Africa, Archbishop Tutu stressed that 'we would want to be among the first to call for the lifting of sanctions', but said the Anglican Church in the Province of Southern Africa had set two conditions of 'dealing effectively with the violence, especially in the black community', and the 'establishment of a transitional government'.

Archbishop Tutu added that 'we are deeply, deeply concerned about the inter-relatedness of things', and recognised that 'it is crucial that the economy take off'. As a Church, he said, 'we would want to look again at what we can do on our part to assist the movement toward normalisation'.

The Story

'The Church obviously has a tremendous influence over the hearts and minds of its members,' De Klerk said, and can help 'bring Christians together, bring leaders together' to reach the majority of moderate South Africans who will support political change.

After meeting with Mangosuthu Buthelezi, leader of the Inkatha Freedom Party, Archbishop Carey said that they 'talked about some of the problems that you are facing here, and the role that your party plays in all this.' The Archbishop noted that Dr Buthelezi is 'a fellow Anglican' and that 'it has been one of my joys coming to South Africa to see the strength of Anglicanism here, its commitment to change and renewal of the life of the country.' Dr Buthelezi said, 'I thank the Archbishop for making it possible for me to meet the spiritual leader of our Anglican Communion and also for the opportunity that I had to discuss formally some of the problems that face this country'. He also said he shared plans for a possible meeting in February with African National Congress leader, Dr Nelson Mandela.

In an address to the joint meeting following the press conference, Dr Buthelezi chided the country's churches for not recognising their own complicity in maintaining apartheid in the past. 'I detect all too frequently . . . a sense of righteousness in which some of our church leaders are claiming the victory of the suffering masses who struggled against apartheid as victories for their advance-guard political thinking.' Instead, he said, 'Let us understand that there is a need for us to look at the reality that the errors of political leaders everywhere imperilled the very souls of men and women, and that the Church was too confused in its thinking to avert the centuries of suffering which mankind has known.'

Dr Buthelezi added that 'that is not to say that the Church leaders have not played their prophetic role through decades of apartheid and oppression,' and pointed to Archbishop Desmond Tutu as an example of that prophetic role of the church.

As one possible positive step, he called for an 'All Church Conference of Review' on the country's situation. The meeting, he suggested, would be 'designed to stop to see where we are, to see how we are blundering, and to see how to move forward. We desperately need the guidance that would come out of such a meeting.'

The Anglican Church has been 'one of the most powerful forces' in supporting the movement towards democratic reform in South Africa, Dr Nelson Mandela, leader of the African National Congress, told the joint meeting. 'The Anglican Church has been in the front lines when our leaders were in jail,' Dr Mandela said. 'It was the Church, the religious groups, that kept these ideas alive.'

As he entered the hall to speak, some of the audience broke into an impromptu song, calling on Dr Mandela to 'lead us to freedom'. He called

Archbishop Carey 'one of the most powerful friends of the democratic forces in this country', Dr Mandela said the Archbishop's 'coming to South Africa has brought him into physical contact with the many problems which are facing our land. Bringing his high office here,' he said, has bolstered 'the morale of our people far beyond the borders of the Anglican Church.'

The resounding call for democratic reform that Archbishop Carey made in his sermon at a massive Eucharist held in Cape Town on 24 January, 'echoed throughout the length and breadth of our country,' Dr Mandela said.

He stressed the Church's role in his own upbringing. 'Our generation is a product of missionary education,' he said. 'We were trained in schools that were run exclusively by the Church. We are therefore proud of the Church, because the little education it gave put us in a better position to serve our people.'

Dr Mandela, who was held as a political prisoner by the South African government for 27 years, told of being held at the Robben Island prison in cold, wet cells with little opportunity for exercise. It was the Church that negotiated for better treatment for prisoners, and which offered hope through the visits of clergy.

'The Church has played a seminal role in the struggle for democracy, and it will continue to play that role,' he said.

Responding to Dr Mandela, Archbishop Carey stressed that 'diversity is a characteristic of Anglicanism,' and that 'underlying it is a passionate commitment to justice and equality and freedom.'

'Your visit to us has made a deep impression,' Archbishop Carey said. 'You are a symbol of the amazing ability of the human spirit to conquer adversity, and to emerge from it.'

'Martin Luther King Jr. said "I have a dream",' Archbishop Carey noted. 'We share your dream of a non-racial, democratic country.'

TOWNSHIP VISITS

The conference spent an entire afternoon having a first-hand look at some of Cape Town's townships and the sprawling shanty towns which have grown up under apartheid.

The Archbishop of Canterbury went to Khayelitsha where he addressed an Anglican gathering on the spot where, a few days before, seven people died in an arson attack. Dr Carey said he hated the kind of system that caused the poverty he saw in Khayelitsha. 'It is wrong for people to live as

The Story

Archbishops Carey and Tutu at Township

you do. I say with tears in my eyes that I almost feel ashamed that I was born with white skin.'

Several members said they had seen worse conditions, for example Smokey Mountain in the Philippines, or Bangkok's notorious slums. What made them indignant was that these conditions had been deliberately created. 'It may be worse in Bangkok,' said Canon Monty Morris. 'But that's no excuse. I am astounded that a political system would make people live like that.'

There were questions, too, about the way police and public officials work. Bishop Paul Reeves said: 'What happened at Khayelitsha the other day was that the police didn't arrive until an hour after the trouble started, despite shootings with carbide and all that sort of thing. It demonstrated the need for independent monitors to ask serious questions of the way the police do their work in South Africa.'

Alongside huge problems which will take more than a generation to solve, there were signs of hope. Not far from Khayelitsha stands the new township of Delft, where residents can choose among a range of houses, and the community is consulted about provision of facilities. The trouble is that people moving in to Delft have sometimes been on waiting lists as long as 20 years.

Standing alone for Peace

The pain of South Africa, at times easy to forget in the beautiful, cosmopolitan setting of Cape Town, was powerfully brought home by the simple but devastating story of one priest and his struggles to curb violence. This story was told during the presentation of the Church of the Province of Southern Africa.

For eight years Archdeacon Elijah Thwala, from the township of Wembezi near Estcourt, Natal, has regularly looked death in the face as he has tried to reconcile followers of the rival Inkatha Freedom Party (IFP) and the African National Congress (ANC).

Since 1992, more than 400 people have died violently in the Natal midlands, known as the 'killing fields' of South Africa. Fr Thwala was frustrated when local politicians refused to join him in meetings. He was even more surprised to be turned down by other church leaders.

'You are on the hit list. You are going to be killed. Do you want us to be killed as well?' they asked. He was left alone to get on with a one man campaign. The post brought 'terrible letters accusing me of getting involved in politics. I was told I must stay in the church and forget about politics while people were dying. Politics was not my game, but I was concerned about the lives of people who were being killed every day.'

Eventually Fr Thwala managed to find two men, Mr T. Nyathi and Mr S. Dlamini, both teachers but neither Christians, to join him. One day a member of the congregation came to warn him that all three were marked for death. 'He cried when I refused to move out. It was a difficult step for me to leave people dying in order to save myself. I just couldn't leave Wembezi.'

With a slow, measured voice, Fr Thwala described waiting that evening. 'Half past seven. I was still at home. The wife of Mr Nyathi phoned. She said "They've killed my husband",' he said. 'At eight o'clock Mr Dlamini's wife phoned. I was still at home. "They have killed my husband".'

Police had come to Fr Thwala's house in time to stop his murder. But the next day nearly 100 people gathered at his gate. 'I knew this was my day,' Fr Thwala said. 'It came to my mind that if I stayed in the house, all of us were going to be killed. The only way was to move out to save my kids, my wife, so that I can be killed but my family left alive.'

Outside the crowd claimed they were looking for an ANC man who had

The Story

run into Fr Thwala's house. They threatened to shoot him if he refused to produce the man. Then, while he was arguing with some of them, Fr Thwala's 13 year-old son came out, worried about his Dad. 'That is the boy,' shouted some of the crowd. But a member of Fr Thwala's congregation who was there shouted, 'No! That is his son. I know him.' With that the crowd left. Fr Thwala had been saved.

Despite great pressures Fr Thwala stayed on for many months. 'I was not looking for martyrdom. No, the love of my people made me stay. It is because I have a message in the time of violence. A message of peace. A message of reconciliation. Even when my ministry was being rejected I felt within me that there was a time when God will come and help me, that this message of reconciliation will be accepted some day.'

Then a fire bomb destroyed his house in July 1992 and he was forced to move from Wembezi to Estcourt, though he continued to visit Wembezi. But then on 9 January, 1993 he finally moved to Durban 'because they were still hunting for me to kill me'. Now the people of Wembezi are without a priest.

PEACE IN MOZAMBIQUE

Many of the countries represented at Cape Town are torn apart by violence. But for the first time in almost a generation, peace reigns in Mozambique. 'The Gospel was the driving force bringing an end to the violence,' said the Bishop of Lebombo, Dinis Sengulane. He went on: 'Mozambique was badly hit by violence for 16 years. About half a million people died and much of the country's infrastructure was destroyed. Most rural districts were inaccessible and over 1000 schools and hostels were closed or destroyed. In the diocese of Lebombo, 59 out of the 109 congregations were dismantled. In Niassa, 60 out of 100. All other Churches experienced similar losses. But, thank God, the violence is over. Peace has been restored. Refugees numbering over one and a half million are returning from neighbouring countries and beyond. Businesses are starting again. The diocese of Lebombo is planning to establish at least 100 congregations by next Advent.'

When asked how peace was achieved he replied: 'The Churches are the Servant of the Prince of Peace. Seeing the suffering of the people, they decided to call both warring factions, namely the government and Renamo, to sit down and talk about their differences. It took about four years to convince them of the wisdom of the need for dialogue. It took another two years to organise negotiations. A year after they had started there had still been no practical results. Then the Church took another step, which was to persuade the President of Mozambique and the President of Renamo to meet personally and set a date for a ceasefire. They signed a Peace Accord in Rome on 4 October, 1992, which ended the violence.'

So is this the end of the story? 'No,' says the Bishop. 'A very important step has been taken, but now there is the need to convert swords into ploughshares. That means disarmament. There is a need to rebuild a shattered economy. To re-shape the human image which has suffered traumas of various kinds.'

THE LOST SHEPHERD

The spontaneous emergence of a 16,000 strong Anglican Church with 90 congregations in war-torn Angola was one of the most interesting stories to surface at the meeting.

The work was begun earlier this century by Archibald Patterson, who founded the United Evangelical Church of Angola. It survived for decades without any contact with the Anglican church. Then in 1990 the remarkable Bishop Dinis Sengulane from Mozambique was invited to Angola by the UEC. He ordained the first clergy, held confirmations and offered pastoral care and teaching.

Though on different sides of Africa, Angola and Mozambique share the Portuguese language in common. Now Angola is recognised as an Archdeaconry and six Angolans are now studying for ordination in the Mozambique capital, Maputo. 'Angola is a parable of the tale of the lost shepherd who is sought and found by his sheep,' Bishop Sengulane says.

STUDENTS LEARN ON THE JOB

Working alongside the official communications team at the Cape Town conference were a group of very enthusiastic trainees from the dioceses of the Church of the Province of Southern Africa. These volunteers lived on campus and joined in with the general panic of the newsroom. The training project was sponsored by Trinity Church, New York City.

At the final press conference of the Joint Meeting, Archbishop Desmond Tutu said the presence of so many delegates from all over the world had been 'a shot in the arm' for the Church of the Province of Southern Africa. The Archbishop of Canterbury said: 'We will go home rather transformed ourselves because in seeing the suffering of your people, we have seen some of the glory as well.'

The Story

Regional Meetings

One of the innovations at the Cape Town meeting was holding a series of regional meetings which enabled delegates to discuss common concerns in depth. It added a new dimension and is sure to become a permanent part of future meetings.

Out of the African regional meeting came resolutions about the suffering caused by the AIDS pandemic and the response of the Churches, and a passionate plea from the Church in the Sudan to enlist the help of the international community to help negotiate an end to a decade of civil war.

Europe's agenda included a review of where Member Churches are on the ordination of women, and response to the Church of England's recent decision to go ahead with this. Ireland and the Lusitanian Church of Portugal have recently agreed to ordain women. In Wales and Scotland the legislative process is under-way. Among the other topics was the impact in the region of the recent visit to Rome by the Archbishop of Canterbury.

One of the major concerns of the East Asia and the Pacific was the appalling human rights situation in Myanmar (formerly Burma), where Anglicans are among those suffering terribly under an unelected regime which has conducted a continuous war against ethnic minorities.

The South Pacific region expressed frustration about how, despite so much public condemnation, the environment continues to be despoiled by foreign interests. Another area of concern was the long-standing crisis in Bougainville, Papua New Guinea. The resulting resolution took the view that Bougainville should remain an integral part of PNG but that peace and human rights must be restored.

The Middle East and Indian Sub Continent region met against the backcloth of the headlines created by Israel's deportation of Palestinians from Gaza and the West Bank and their suffering from exposure and hunger, trapped in the Lebanese border region. There was a plea to all Member Churches to do their utmost to enable justice and peace to prevail in lands sacred to Christianity, Islam and Judaism. Another concern was pastoral care of expatriate families and the problems caused by fundamentalist groups.

The Americas region had a lively discussion over the future of the Lambeth Conference. They discussed West Indies clergy drain, a problem raised by the Province which is vulnerable to losing clergy to mainland North America. Concern was expressed for the Church and people of Haiti, whose democratically elected government was recently overthrown, accompanied by serious violations of human rights. Another topic which produced a spirited debate was the question of the Church's attitude to homosexuality.

The Anglican Vision

THE DYNAMICS OF COMMUNION

'Communion is a divine calling because it is of the essence of God. Therefore the search for communion is one of our most fundamental tasks. To speak of the dynamics of communion is to speak of something fundamental about ourselves and about God.' — Archbishop Michael Peers.

Since the first Lambeth Conference in 1867 the Anglicans have been engaged together in exploring the meaning of communion, exploring in human communion what we know of God through the revelation of God in Jesus Christ.

The Anglican understanding of communion is dynamic, never static. It has been given expression in Anglicanism through many different cultural assumptions and forms. It has been given shape by the Anglican response to different needs and challenges throughout history. It has required Anglicans to express ancient words in new ways. It is both an eternal calling and a present search.

On the issue of communion and its dynamics the meeting had two particular purposes:

- to strengthen communion by considering further the question of Anglican identity and the exercise of authority in the Anglican Communion; and
- to nourish growth in communion with ecumenical partners at all levels and to identify new initiatives.

The meeting had the benefit of an address on the Anglican vision of communion by the Revd Dr John Pobee, a West African Anglican from the staff of the World Council of Churches. One of the themes traced was the translation of Anglicanism from English origins to other parts of the world.

He left delegates with five questions for consideration:

- is there any continuing value of 'Englishness' in the contemporary, world-wide Communion?
- has the Communion sufficiently broken out of its original 'Englishness' to reflect and appropriate other cultures which have come on board?
- is there some common thread which runs through the entire Anglican traditions in all their local manifestations, whether Ghana, England, South Africa, Myanmar, Aotearoa, or the USA?
- is there evidence that the Communion remains in 'Anglo-Saxon captivity' and if so, is this detrimental to its mission today?

The Story

- do Anglican churches – consciously or unconsciously – hold an 'establishment' view of themselves?

THE ORDINATION OF WOMEN

During the past decade and a half, the ordination of women in an increasing number of Member Churches has proved a crucial test for the Anglican understanding of communion. Since the 1988 Lambeth Conference the position has become even more complex because women have been elected bishops in two Anglican Provinces. Most recently the Churches in Australia and England and Ireland had agreed to ordain women priests.

The main catalysts for discussion at Cape Town were two letters to the Archbishop of Canterbury. The first was from the International Bishops' Conference on Faith and Order, a group of 50 bishops who met in London in June 1992. The second was from traditionalists in the USA, expressing concern about expectations that one of their number, the Revd Jack Iker, a well-known opponent of women's ordination, would not receive enough votes from the American Bishops to confirm his election as bishop coadjutor of the Diocese of Fort Worth. Traditionalists claimed that failure to confirm Fr Iker would proclaim in effect 'that there is no longer any room for those who deny or are unable to affirm the ordination of women'. Both groups asked in effect for consideration of an extra-territorial or even extra-provincial jurisdiction for the pastoral care of those with doctrinal objections to the ordination of women. As it turned out, by the time the Joint Meeting began, Fr Iker was within two votes of obtaining Standing Committee consent, and the Presiding Bishop of ECUSA said he expected his election to be ratified by the House of Bishops.

These issues were discussed both by the joint meeting's Dynamics of Communion Working Group and by the Primates. The outcome of all the discussions was a firm 'no' to the call for separate jurisdictions.

The meeting reaffirmed Resolution 72 of the 1988 Lambeth Conference which calls for 'respect for diocesan boundaries and the authority of bishops within these boundaries'. The same resolution declared that it is 'deemed inappropriate behaviour for any bishop or priest of this Communion to exercise episcopal or pastoral authority within a diocese without first obtaining the permission and invitation of the ecclesial authority thereof'.

The meeting called on bishops from throughout the Anglican Communion 'to be scrupulously fair in their pastoral care of those who oppose and those who cannot accept the ordination of women'. At the same time it asked the Archbishop of Canterbury to reconvene his Commission

The Anglican Vision

on Women in the Episcopate, otherwise known as the Eames Commission, which is chaired by the Most Revd Robert Eames of Ireland.

Anglicans have, on occasion, allowed non-territorial bishoprics to accommodate mission to people with a substantially different culture, for example the Maori diocese of Aotearoa in New Zealand or the Order of Ethiopia in Southern Africa. But according to Bishop Mark Dyer (USA), a member of the Eames Commission, Anglicans resisted parallel jurisdictions, taking as the precedent Canon 8 of the Council of Nicea which affirmed the integrity of the diocese and the diocesan bishop. 'Any kind of extra-territorial jurisdiction would in fact be schism.'

For Fr John Broadhurst, a leading English opponent of the ordination of women, parallel jurisdictions need not add up to schism. 'Schism is surely living apart. What traditionalists are seeking is a means for living together.' Bishop Colin James (England), who had participated both in the International Faith and Order conference and in preparation of the statement issued by the House of Bishops of the Church of England about the pastoral care of opponents, said his concern was to maintain 'interim arrangements to help people live side by side'.

Some traditionalists, he said, were worried at what they saw as increasing signs of 'a new orthodoxy test' which seemed to say 'unless you consent to the ordination of women you can't be ordained or you can't be a bishop'. He said he hoped the decisions of the meeting would be seen as a clear signal to traditionalists that 'we hear what you are saying' and that they are 'still regarded as loyal Anglicans in good standing, and that our position is an acceptable theological position to hold'.

DOCTRINAL COMMISSION

The joint meeting agreed to ask the Archbishop of Canterbury to set up a new Inter-Anglican Theological and Doctrinal Commission. It received the report of an international doctrinal consultation which met at the Virginia Theological Seminary in 1992 and produced a report, 'Belonging Together', which was commended for further study by Member Churches. The meeting put on record its thanks to the Virginia Seminary for its generous financial support of the 1992 meeting.

INTER-FAITH DIALOGUE

Growing numbers of Member Churches are involved in Inter-Faith discussions. The 1988 Lambeth Conference (Resolutions 20 and 21) encouraged the process and suggested an Inter-Faith Committee to help ensure a

The Story

common approach by Anglicans. It also encouraged close links with the work of the World Council of Churches in this field.

The joint meeting agreed to set up a world-wide network of correspondents, with representatives from each Member Church. The network will be serviced through the new Centre for Anglican Communion Studies, which opened in October 1992 and is based at the CMS and USPG colleges at Selly Oak, Birmingham, England. It also accepted the offer of the Bishop of Lichfield of part-time help from his Inter-Faith Officer, the Revd Nigel Pounde, who will convene the network.

LITURGY

Celebrating the vision
'The Church's liturgy is the way by which it describes and celebrates its vision. Through mission we bear witness to Jesus Christ who has proclaimed the Kingdom or reign of God and taught his disciples to pray for its coming. When we assemble for worship, we recall and recite what God has done in the lives of his people now and throughout history. In doing so we begin to learn the life-style of the Kingdom.' *[Paul Gibson – from an unpublished paper.]*

Should young children have communion alongside their parents in Anglican churches? What is the precise meaning and place of confirmation in the Anglican understanding of Christian initiation? Must confirmation always be administered by bishops? Should Anglicanism take steps to revive the Catechumenate to instruct its people in the essentials of the faith?

These were just some of the issues which came before the joint meeting from the International Anglican Liturgical Consultation held in Toronto in 1991. The meeting recommended serious study of 'Walk in Newness of Life', the report of the Consultation.

Members took the opportunity to share information about the progress of liturgical revision in their Churches. Some were concerned that more information should be shared. People wanted to know more about the impact of the Decade of Evangelism on liturgies. They also wanted to keep abreast of the way individual Member Churches are dealing with inculturation – the way in which the universal elements of liturgy are adapted so that they communicate meaningfully in the local situation. It was therefore proposed that the Secretariat should distribute a regular newsletter to keep Member Churches informed of developments throughout the world.

While affirming the need for the liturgy to communicate meaningfully through the culture and thought forms of local people who use it, some members were concerned to make sure that new liturgies retain a recognisable Anglican liturgical form and outline. In the light of this discussion the Meeting asked for educational material to be prepared to help Member Churches in their understanding of the universal elements of Anglican liturgy as described by the 1988 Lambeth Conference. These elements included: the public reading of the Scriptures in the language of the people and instruction based on them; the use of the two dominical sacraments (Baptism and Holy Communion); episcopal ordination of all three Orders of Ministry with the laying on of hands; public recitation and teaching of the Apostles and Nicene Creeds.

By far the most lively liturgical debate occurred when the Liturgical Working Group brought forward principles and criteria to be used by Member Churches as they consider whether particular godly men and women should be remembered in Church calendars. The document was careful not to appear to be endorsing creation of a list of Anglican saints. And it sought to make the point that we are not celebrating these people as such but 'Christ in them . . . and consequently "Christ in us the hope of glory".'

Nevertheless, the suggestion succeeded in bringing out the differences in perception that still exist among Anglicans over these kinds of issues. The sticking point came particularly where the statement of Criteria and Principles spoke of how 'the first step in a process of commemoration is the spontaneous devotion of people who knew the person involved and testify to his/her holiness'. Was there a danger of devotion to particular people taking the place of due devotion to Christ? This was a concern expressed by some delegates – though not all – from predominantly Roman Catholic countries where Anglicanism is presented a clear alternative.

The set of Principles and Criteria went through with only slight amendment. The debate itself was one of those moments when some of the differences of outlook between the different traditions in Anglicanism come out into the open.

ECUMENISM

Jesus prayed (John 17.20-21) for his disciples 'that they all may be one, as you, Father, are in me and I in you . . . so that the world might believe'. For a long time the modern ecumenical movement expressed its response to Jesus' prayer by working for 'organic unity' between the various Churches.

However, as we all know, over the decades the quest for organic unity has proved much more difficult than was first expected. Moreover, as the

The Story

various unity negotiations progressed, there was a realisation that the vision of a single, world-wide Church left out something vital. As well as presenting a unified face to the world there was a need to recognise and celebrate the richness and diversity of the traditions of individual churches.

The result has been a change in emphasis. Instead of concentrating on structural unity negotiations, ecumenism today emphasises the need for Christians to grow together in their understanding and practice of their faith.

Much of the official ecumenical work of the Anglican Communion therefore has three main strands:

- working towards agreement in faith, in official conversations with other Churches and Communions;
- working towards interchangeability of ministries with Churches and Communions who already work alongside Anglicans, and with whom we already share a lot in common;
- working in partnership with other Christian Churches in mission, evangelism, and social witness.

So when the Joint Meeting came to discussing ecumenism its first act was to state its commitment to continue to work for the unity of all Christians and to work on those issues which prevent the Churches coming together.

It then went on to review relations between the Anglican Communion to the World Council of Churches and other key Churches where there is an official commitment to theological discussions and joint action.

The World Council of Churches
While there has been a Primates' meeting since the Seventh Assembly of the WCC in Canberra, this was the first time the ACC had an opportunity to respond to it. Events have moved rapidly in the WCC since Canberra. The WCC is now engaged in a radical review of its role and structures. There is a new General Secretary, Dr Konrad Raiser, and he is gathering around him an almost completely new senior staff team.

Anglicans were at the forefront of the creation of the WCC and almost all the Provinces of the Anglican Communion are full members. It is vital that Anglicans play their full part in its life and co-operate fully in the review process.

The Joint Meeting reaffirmed its support of the World Council of Churches (WCC). It called on Member Churches to respond seriously to a new study book, *Understanding the Vision of the WCC*, which will be distributed during 1993. It agreed to set up a small working group to study the relationship between the Anglican Communion and the WCC and report back through the ACC.

Roman Catholic relations
The whole tone of relations between the Anglicans and the Roman Catholic Church has been affected by the Vatican response to the first Anglican-Roman Catholic International Commission (ARCIC). Representatives in Cape Town were frank in expressing disappointment.

People strongly committed to a cause will always try to put the best possible face on setbacks. And those specially committed to relations with the Roman Catholic Church were doing that at Cape Town. Nevertheless there were developments which were a source of genuine encouragement.

In recent years in a number of places throughout the Anglican Communion, local links with Roman Catholics have been strengthened. In Canada, for instance, there is an annual meeting between the Anglican and Roman Catholic bishops. In England, the Anglican and Roman Catholic bishops of the City of Liverpool work together very closely and as a matter of policy issue joint statements on social issues, together with the local leader of the Methodist Church. The ecumenical working group at Cape Town heard reports of local developments in areas such as inter-church families, joint clergy conferences, joint theological education, as well as shared witness and community service.

The Joint Meeting resisted calls to bring reflection on these local developments into the life of ARCIC. It will continue to work on its existing brief, seeking to resolve the theological differences which divided the two Churches from the time of the Reformation.

Oriental Orthodox relations
Oriental Orthodox Churches are vulnerable communities. In many countries they live as a Christian minority alongside Islam. Their isolation from other Christian communities can be traced to early church history and the refusal of their forebears to agree to the Canons of the Council of Chalcedon, 451, which declared the two natures of Christ.

For many years Anglicans have built links with these Churches through the Anglican/Oriental Orthodox Forum. Relations with these Churches have also changed as a result of many of their peoples now living alongside Western Christians in cities like Sydney and Melbourne.

The Joint Meeting encouraged the Anglican/Oriental Orthodox Forum to work on a joint statement on the doctrine of the nature of Christ, in order to

The Story

create a basis for better relations in the future, both with the Anglican Communion and the wider community of Churches.

Baptist relations
There are Baptists in many countries world-wide, including large numbers in the former Soviet Union. They are linked together through the Baptist World Alliance. The 1988 Lambeth Conference called for official dialogue between Anglicans and the Baptists, but this has so far been prevented because of lack of funds. This situation has not yet changed.

The Joint Meeting in Cape Town therefore encouraged continuation of local contacts between Anglicans and Baptists. It felt that Anglicans could learn much from reports emerging from official dialogue between Baptists and other Christian Churches. In addition it saw the need for more thought about how representatives go about the process of dialogue, bearing in mind, for example, that a debate exists between some Baptist communities about the inspiration and authority of Scripture.

Orthodox relations
The winds of change in the former Soviet Union and Eastern bloc countries have radically changed the tempo of official relations between Anglicans and the Eastern Orthodox Churches. For Anglicans, relations with the Orthodox has suddenly become one of the most hopeful fronts for inter-church co-operation.

Up until 1990 the major Anglican objective for Orthodox relations was pastoral, encouraging Churches living day to day under atheistic Communist regimes. Now there is unprecedented opportunity for Anglicans to offer material aid and practical help to strengthen these churches.

There are great stresses on the Orthodox Churches in this new situation. They are now being called on to undertake things which have not been allowed for 70 years, e.g. re-establishing parishes and pastoral care, providing social services and education. Their financial resources are stretched. And they have suddenly found that they do not possess the know-how to fulfil many of these tasks.

What is more, the winds of change have unleashed a whole wave of secularism. In addition, cults and 'new age' practices are growing apace. Many Western groups are flooding into the former Eastern bloc to conduct evangelistic work, sometimes in ways which are insensitive to the local culture and to local Christian communities.

The Orthodox Churches are therefore looking specially to Anglicanism to help with theological resources and scholarships. They are also seeking practical advice on how to develop the work of the Church in this new context. So, for example, the Patriarch of Moscow recently asked the House of Bishops of the Episcopal Church USA to send some of its number to offer training about the role of a modern bishop.

Old Catholic relations
The Old Catholic Churches, which exist mainly in Western Europe and the USA, grew up during the last century in protest against what were considered unacceptable developments in the Roman Catholic Church. These Churches have been in full communion with the Anglican Communion for over 60 years.

A new impetus has been given to Old Catholic relations as a result of recent political changes in Western Europe. In 1992 the Single European Act, which was accepted by the countries of the European Community, came into full effect. This new situation is challenging the Churches of

The Old Catholic Archbishop with the Bishop of Portugal (left)

The Story

Europe to build closer links and to work together in evangelism and social witness.

The Joint Meeting at Cape Town agreed to set up an Anglican/Old Catholic International Co-ordinating Council to build on these opportunities.

Lutheran relations
Close relations exist between Anglican and Lutheran Churches in many places throughout the world. In Europe and the USA the two Churches have entered into agreements to work more closely. For many years the Church of England and the Church of Sweden have been linked in a form of communion. Now plans are under way to build on this commitment in order to achieve full communion. And as well as including the Churches of England and Sweden, the relationship is being widened. It will include all the Anglican Churches in the British Isles: Ireland, Scotland and Wales. And it will include the Lutheran Churches of the Baltic region (Latvia, Estonia and Lithuania) and the remaining Nordic Lutheran Churches (Finland, Iceland, Norway and Denmark).

To complete the process a theological study is required to explore how the various agreements achieved so far with these Churches affect the Anglican Communion as a whole.

The methodology of ecumenical dialogue
There has been much talk of a 'winter in ecumenism'. Yet despite the many difficulties which plague the ecumenical movement, there are still many encouraging stories of how local churches are working together, and how ecumenical covenants are flourishing.

The difficulties which the ecumenical movement currently faces are prompting a lot of soul searching, in particular about the methodology which underlies ecumenical dialogue. One important issue, for example, is the way in which Scripture is interpreted. Another is the place of the historic documents of participating Churches, including what we mean when we ask whether an ecumenical agreement is 'consonant' with the faith of our particular Church. Another issue is how what has been agreed in official dialogues is to be communicated and 'owned' in the respective Churches.

The Anglican Centre in Rome
The Anglican Centre in Rome was founded shortly after the historic meet-

ing between Archbishop Michael Ramsey and Pope Paul VI in 1963. The Centre exists to help make Anglicanism more widely known within the central structures of the Roman Catholic Church. It operates a substantial reference library on Anglican history and doctrine.

For many years it was supported financially through the Inter-Anglican budget, but in recent years it has been decided that it should be funded independently. There is currently an appeal to raise an endowment of £1.5 million to enable the Centre to be self-supporting. The Joint Meeting agreed to lend its support to the appeal.

Churches of Bangladesh, India and Pakistan
Former Anglicans now form part of the united Churches of the Indian subcontinent. These Churches have always been part of the Anglican Consultative Council, and in 1988 bishops from these Churches were invited to attend the Lambeth Conference.

It has been widely agreed that international Anglican meetings and commissions have been much enriched by the contributions of representatives from these Churches and the Joint Meeting agreed that efforts should be made to include these Churches on such bodies as the Ecumenical Advisory Group and the Inter-Anglican Theological and Doctrinal Commission.

The date of Easter
For hundreds of years one of the symbols of Christian disunity has been a failure of the Eastern and Western Churches to agree a common date for Easter. Now that many Eastern and Western Churches have closer links, particularly through the movements of peoples to countries such as the USA and Australia where the two traditions live side by side, coming to an agreement about this matter is no longer as impossible as it once was. That is not to say that obtaining agreement will necessarily be easy. There are 14 different self-governing Orthodox Churches which will all need to be part of an accord. The Joint Meeting nevertheless encouraged the Churches of East and West to continue their efforts to find a common date for Easter.

SHARING AND SUFFERING

At Cape Town delegates shared both their joys and their hardships. Archbishop Amos Waiaru, of Melanesia, came to Cape Town just a few days after Cyclone Nina struck the Solomon Islands on 8 January. The

The Story

Archbishop was on holiday on his own island of Santa Anna when the cyclone hit. 'I spent hours trying to rescue the old people and the children. On two occasions I was almost blown away myself. It was a most frightening experience,' he said.

Cyclone Nina has left a grim toll of destruction throughout the islands and atolls of Temotu Diocese. Three-quarters of the people are homeless. Emergency rations are needed for the next six months while they work on clearing, replanting and harvesting. As yet there are no exact figures for the numbers of people killed in the disaster. Earliest information suggested a figure of around 22 but it is feared many more may have died.

The Church in Melanesia is vigorous and strong with six dioceses, all led by local bishops. Half the dioceses were affected by Cyclone Nina. Some 60 church buildings were lost. There is an urgent need for supplies of prayer and hymn books, Bibles, altar linen, vestments and communion vessels. At Cape Town a special collection was taken to help the Church in Melanesia.

Patrick Forbes

OUR PEOPLE IN PORTUGAL

The Lusitanian Church of Portugal is only 113 years old but is fiercely independent and autonomous. According to Bishop Soares, its bishop, it was formed as a movement against some of the unacceptable dogmas pronounced by the Vatican during the nineteenth century.

'We were greatly influenced by two great Irish theologians in those early days, Lord Plunkett, who consecrated many of our churches and Archbishop John Gregg, who ordained my predecessor to the priesthood.' The Archbishop of Canterbury is the Church's Metropolitan.

It has 5,000 members, scattered throughout the whole of Portugal. It has an important ecumenical role. 'Last year I was invited by my Roman Catholic counterparts to celebrate the eucharist in a Dominican church and that is not an isolated incident.' Last year, during the celebrations for the 500th anniversary of Columbus, the Portuguese Council of Churches issued an open letter to the President of the Republic of Portugal affirming their pride in their national hero but recognising that cultural mistakes were made. It said that apologies were due to indigenous people.

Bishop Soares, who himself combines his episcopal role with a high-powered position in a national bank, is very positive about the role of the laity. 'Laity are the future of the church. We must prepare them to take responsibilities. I and most of my clergy are non-stipendiary, I am a banker, others are teachers, fishermen and accountants. That is why I take the role of the laity so seriously. Under these clerical robes of mine there is a lay person. For the last three years we have had no candidates for the ministry, so we have devised a new structure for parish ministry. The functions have been divided so that clergy concentrate on sacramental and pastoral work. Administration is now in the hands of a Vestry President, and this post is open to lay men and women.'

The Lusitanian Church voted to ordain women in 1990. So far none have been ordained, although there are four women Lay Readers and the way is open for them to be ordained in the future. The Lusitanian Church, made up entirely of Portuguese, lives alongside Church of England Chaplaincies which form part of the diocese of Europe. It has evolved its own particular style and tradition. He deeply values the links with the Church world-wide which come as a result of being part of the Anglican Communion. 'It is so important to be identified with our world-wide brothers and sisters.'

The public profile of the Lusitanian Church is out of all proportion to its size. 'Last year one of the national daily newspapers ran a series on influential religious personalities,' says Bishop Soares, 'and would you believe it they started with me!'

CLOBBERED FOR CHRIST

Unless a Church is a suffering Church, it can never be the Church of Jesus Christ. Let me give you what is just an arbitrary list. The Presiding Bishop and his Church in the United States, standing almost alone against the euphoria of attacking Iraq, are clobbered. Michael Peers and the Anglican Church of Canada, taking a stand on the side of the native people, gets clobbered. The Church in the UK determined to stand together with the coal miners, gets clobbered. The Church in Kenya, speaking out against the oppressiveness of one party rule, gets clobbered. The same with the Church in Malawi. The Church in Japan when it says 'no' to emperor worship. It isn't, it seems, a coincidence that witness, suffering and martyrdom go together. There can be no glory any other way.
Archbishop Desmond Tutu. Extracted from his sermon at the opening Eucharist.

THE ANGUISH OF DIVISION

'Brazil is a country of continental size. It is multi-racial and multi-cultural. The gap between the wealthy minority and the vast poor majority is acute. At ecumenical gatherings we can't celebrate the Eucharist. This causes a lot of anguish because people really believe the Eucharist is the bread of life

The Story

and the power for unity.' This anguish was expressed by a Roman Catholic bishop who recently hosted the Eighth National Meeting of Base Communities on the outskirts of Rio de Janeiro.

It was an evening. Some 2,000 people who came from all over Brazil gathered at the Public Square for the celebration of the anniversary of the diocese. The bishop invited a Presbyterian to preach, myself to bless the bread to be shared and a Methodist woman minister to give the final benediction.

After the joy of exchanging the peace, with all the exuberance of Latin Americans, this bishop said that we would like to celebrate the Eucharist together, but because of church regulations we can't. 'But in the hope that one day we can celebrate together, I hand this stole to Bishop Sumio.' He reached out and put it on my neck. And he gave me his cross as well.

Another time our House of Bishops had decided to hold a retreat in a Roman Catholic house in Porto Alegre and had invited a Roman Catholic bishop to speak to us. He accepted the invitation. When we talked about our Eucharistic celebration he said the chapel was available. 'I will be

The Primate of Brazil

there,' he said. 'But you know I can't communicate. However the sisters will come and I have authorised them to communicate.'

Then one of the nuns came with a packet of wafers to be consecrated because there was a shortage of priests. So for several days the nuns had reserved sacraments consecrated by Anglican bishops.

In one diocese a young deacon was sent to a mission station in a small town because there was no priest available to run the mission. At seminary the deacon had learned the importance of the Eucharist. As Holy Week and Easter approached he tried to find someone to consecrate the elements. First he talked to the Methodist clergy, but they were unwilling. So he went to the Roman Catholic parish. By then it was already Maundy Thursday and time to start the Mass. The priest agreed to consecrate the elements and invited him to preach. So the young deacon read the Gospel and shared a meditation. For his part the priest was delighted. It wasn't very often that he had the help of a deacon!

For all that, I do not expect this peculiar crossing over the official boundaries happens in many other parts of the world.
Bishop Sumio Takatsu, Brazil

SHARING THE WORK AT HOME IS BASIC

At one of the assemblies of the Basic Communities near Brasilia, everybody, including the bishops, had to wash their own dishes. A couple who came from a region where male dominance is strong told us that as a result of the Bible study they are now participating equally between men and women.

In the past this couple used to go out into the field together to work. At noon they came back together. While the wife was cooking the husband would rest. After the meal, while the wife washed up the husband would take a nap. Now that has all changed. And the local priest has started ordering husbands to wash dishes for 15 days as penance instead of the traditional 15 Hail Marys and the Lord's Prayer! I told this story to a clergy conference. Some of those who came from rural areas and worked in the fields had red faces.
Bishop Sumio Takatsu, Brazil

✢

The Most Revd George Browne

Mission and Evangelism

'We must turn the Church inside out. The Church must begin to live on the outside of itself. What is the sign of a dying Church? It's when the organism is replaced by organisation. It's when survival becomes our overwhelming concern. Look at the budget of any Church organisation and see what it's spending on mission, young people, young adults, Sunday schools, and the wider community. Compare that to what it's spending on itself and then you'll get a measure of whether its declining, standing still or growing.' *Archbishop George Carey.*

✚

'The good news is that people still need God. The bad news is that there's no simple solution to how we communicate. The E word is not an easy word. And I'm rather glad it isn't because human nature does not come ready-made like a factory product. We are unique creatures, with precious qualities that cannot be cribbed, cabined, or confined.' *Archbishop George Carey.*

✚

Few Lambeth Conference resolutions have caught the Anglican imagination in quite the same way as Lambeth 88's call for a Decade of Evangelism in the run up to the end of the millennium. There are abundant signs of the impact of this call on the life of our churches.

There has already been a massive switch from maintenance to mission. Churches were becoming engaged in deliberate, planned and sustained endeavours to reach out, both to the lapsed and those without Christian faith. In the process many of them were being changed as they saw the need to make their worship more 'user friendly', and to train up their people so that they were confident to share their faith.

In the first of two addresses to the Joint Meeting, the Archbishop of Canterbury reminded delegates that evangelism 'springs from the nature of God whose desire is that all should know and love him'. He drew a distinction between 'Macro' and 'Micro' evangelism.

'Macro' evangelism is the action of God in history and in the work of Christ, redeeming the world and transforming it. This understanding provided a warrant for the Church to be engaged in 'Kingdom' issues: justice, peace, the environment, freedom and equality. 'Micro' evangelism is the

The Story

action of the Church under the direction of the Holy Spirit, bringing the truth of Christ to each particular generation.

There was no such thing as culture-free evangelism. All of us bring our particular background, experiences and the dominant cultural 'mores' which have shaped us. 'Culture shapes the human voice which answers the voice of Christ.'

One of the great challenges to the Churches, he said, was the impact of urbanisation. It meant a shift from stable to transitory life styles, which in turn undermined a sense of community. Since the Church is strongest where there is community, how is it to act when it is absent? Another challenge was the breakdown of 'Modernism' within the Western world, a loss of confidence in science and rationality which were the inheritance of the Enlightenment. And yet religion was not dying out. Both Islam and Christianity have grown rapidly during this century.

The Church needed to strengthen its confidence in the Gospel. 'To be a Christian is to have a story to relate. Have Western Christians lost the art of story-telling? Has our faith become so cerebral that we have lost the experience?' Was there something here for the Churches of the South to teach the Churches of the North?

REVITALISING THE LOCAL CHURCH

i) The starting point is defining clear objectives. The problem was that so few churches set clear goals for themselves. If you aim for nothing you are sure to get it. Vestries need to agree their own targets, which might include: congregational growth, education of the faithful, unlocking lips, finding out the needs of the community, raising giving.

ii) Developing the talents of the laity is crucial. This means abandonment of the 'one man band' approach to ministry.

iii) Revitalising worship. Worship is the church's shop window, but the common cry of so many people, particularly the young, is that it is 'boring'. Too much worship is too long, old fashioned, and unrelated to people's lives. Worship is not the same as evangelism. Nevertheless it can be a step along the way for people seeking God.

iv) Inviting people to join. Fellowship is a universal need. People all desire to belong.

✝

Bishop Michael Nazir-Ali addresses the conference

MISSION

The keynote for the mission section of the Conference's work was struck by Bishop Michael Nazir-Ali whose theme was Communion and Commission. The principle of partnership was a hallmark of the Early Church. It included church to church support and support of a circle of people.

'In the Anglican Communion, both the MRI (Mutual Responsibilty and Interdependence) and PIM (Partners in Mission) processes have emphasised church to church partnership. If it is the only thing the ACC has achieved, then it is enough. But it does not take account of all the rest: support of people and voluntary bodies.' Having developed church to church partnership, was it now time for the Anglican Communion to think about developing these other areas?

One of the key reasons why Christianity took root throughout the Roman Empire was that Christians were keen travellers. Think of how many different times Priscilla and Aquila appear in the New Testament record. The same can be said of the evangelisation of Britain. As Archbishop Matthew Parker records, roaming was a fundamental part of Celtic Christianity. And as Celtic Christians roamed they began to discover its relationship to mission and it became intentional. So we have the stories of Columba, Aidan, Chad and Patrick, and the traditions of Lindisfarne, Iona and Downpatrick.

According to Bishop Michael Nazir-Ali, under the providence of God, the displacement of people is becoming a significant force in creating the church among peoples who used to be unreachable. One striking example is in the Sudan, where experts identify seven separate reasons why large numbers are being displaced, yet the church there has grown.

At the Joint Meeting of the Primates and ACC at Cape Town, the new Province of Zaire was there in its own right for the first time. This Church was much strengthened by the presence of Christians who fled from Uganda during the Amin days.

Another up-to-date example is what is happening among Iranians. The displacement of thousands of Iranians to cities like London, New York, Sydney and Melbourne has opened up opportunities that were not possible previously. There are now thriving Iranian churches in these cities, and this will duly have an impact back home in Iran.

Bishop Nazir-Ali commented that traditionally the Great Commission is normally read as an imperative, 'Go'. But it could equally be translated 'Having gone'. Now, as over the centuries, Christians finding themselves in

The Story

some new place have discovered remarkable opportunities to share the Gospel that could never have occurred through a planned missionary movement.

+

MISAG

The meeting noted with approval the work of the final meeting of the Mission Issues and Strategy Advisory Group (MISAG), called for its translation into the major languages used throughout the Anglican Communion, and commended it for wider study. It agreed to set up a Mission Commission, to be called Missio, which will:

- be a forum for mission issues;
- develop theological perspectives for mission and evangelism for the Communion;
- encourage new mission structures;
- develop partnership between churches;
- maintain an overview of the Partners-in-Mission process;
- develop the Decade of Evangelism;
- continue developing the database begun by the Mission Agencies' Working Group (MAWG);
- follow up the proposed 'Anglican Encounter in the South' conference in 1993 or 1994;
- prepare for and follow up the projected 'Movement for Mission' conference in 1996;
- report to and receive relevant items from the ACC; and
- support the work of the ACC's mission and evangelism secretary.

The Joint Meeting also asked that the original vision of Partners-in-Mission as an on-going process of mutuality and interdependence be recovered and re-emphasised, 'in place of the current rather expensive and often burdensome one-off consultation approach'.

MISAG II noted that there was 'a growing sense of consultation fatigue and a danger of the PIM Consultation running out of steam'.

THE UNITED NATIONS

The meeting commended the work of the Anglican Observer at the United Nations and recommended that the office be maintained, and that a suitable replacement be found for Sir Paul Reeves when he leaves the post to return to New Zealand at the end of 1993.

YOUTH CONFERENCE

Having expressed regret at the cancellation of an International Youth Conference, planned for Canada in 1993, the meeting agreed a plan to resuscitate the Youth Network and, if possible, reconvene the Conference at a later date. It urged the Anglican Communion to give a high priority to youth work.

PEACE PRIZE

Probably the most exciting new idea to emerge from the meeting was the recommendation that the Archbishop of Canterbury should offer an annual Peace Prize for those who have done outstanding work as peacemakers.

PARTNERSHIP TO FIGHT AIDS

When a World Health Organisation official spoke at a fringe meeting at the 1988 Lambeth Conference, he chided the bishops for not putting AIDS on the agenda. 'Next time you meet it could be your only agenda item,' he said.

Even in 1988 many of the bishops from Africa were denying that there was a disease called AIDS. 'Even myself, I was one of those,' said the Most Revd Yona Okoth, Archbishop of Uganda. 'I did not know that this disease existed in Uganda.' Now, Archbishop Okoth has become a leader in urging the worldwide Anglican Communion to make the international crisis a major priority.

Representatives of African nations presented a successful resolution to the joint conference of the Anglican Consultative Council and the Anglican Communion's Primates, meeting in Cape Town, that called for a universal response to AIDS. Even more, however, the leaders of every African nation represented at the meeting have pledged to try to set up AIDS programmes within their provinces. Archbishop of Canterbury George Carey has agreed to serve on the international advisory board that will help co-ordinate the programmes. The Revd Canon John Lathrop, executive secretary of the Church Commissioners for the Province of the Church of Uganda, was influential in persuading the other African countries to join in the effort to address the continent's AIDS crisis. He will be approaching

Archbishop Okoth

potential financial donors on behalf of the countries, and helping the provinces establish their programmes.

The education about the AIDS situation that Lathrop presented at the meeting was critical, said Archbishop Manasses Kuria of Kenya. Any number of the African delegates 'will go home and say he has heard about AIDS, and if he wasn't talking about AIDS when he came, he will go back talking about AIDS', he said. 'I don't think there is any country that can say it's safe, It took a long time for people to know that there was such a disease as AIDS. So people have died and people were infected long before they knew about it.'

The resolution approved by the meeting urges 'all governments, all Churches, all religious bodies to do all in their power to fight this killer of our people. We endorse and support the work of HIV/AIDS education and prevention throughout the Anglican Communion both locally and internationally. The problem is so vast there is room for every programme.' The resolution also chides governments that are not willing to admit the extent of the disease's inroads in their countries. 'We urge them to disclose the facts regarding HIV/AIDS in their respective countries as a first step towards developing the measures and means necessary to deal with this disease,' the resolution states.

Seven African Primates signed an agreement to work together to fight the AIDS pandemic. The move was welcomed by other African delegates including Nigerian layman Mr Justice Abimbola: 'The Church is always interested in the welfare of the general community. If we are interested in spreading the Gospel which brings life, we certainly should be interested in fighting a disease which destroys and brings death.'

The Ugandan programme of education and prevention, which was developed as an international partnership with the Episcopal Church (USA), the United States Agency for International Development and agencies of the United Nations, was endorsed by the Joint Meeting's resolution in particular as a model for the rest of the Church.

'We note with great joy and gratitude the expressed willingness of the Church of Uganda to respond to requests from other provinces for technical assistance in developing programmes,' the resolution states.

According to Canon Lathrop, in 1992, 32 per cent of all adults in the capital of Kampala who were tested, tested positive for HIV, and, as of January 1993, 31.8 per cent of the young women between 15 and 19 who were tested in greater Kampala are HIV-infected. 'At Makerere University [the country's largest university], the newest job is of coffin-maker to serve the student body,' Lathrop said. 'I don't know of any priest in Uganda who doesn't have a close relative who has died of AIDS.'

With Canon Lathrop's help, a major AIDS conference was held in Mukono, Uganda, in August 1991. 'They don't talk about sexuality in

The Story

Uganda, at least not in the old days, so this was a major breakthrough,' Canon Lathrop said. 'It galvanised the Church in Uganda.'

'It was the first time we talked about sex,' agreed Archbishop Okoth. 'It was the first time we talked about condoms. It was not easy. But the fact was that our clergy were tired of burying the dead from this disease. So we opened our heart and said we needed to know more about this.'

'The formal moral shame that people were concerned about has been getting washed away,' Canon Lathrop said. 'The denial was beginning to erode away. They saw it wasn't just a health problem or a moral problem, but a problem affecting society.'

The potential impact of the Anglican Church in Uganda is great, since it already can claim six million members, about a third of the nation's total population.

✝

WORSHIP HAS DRAWING POWER

Worship has its own 'drawing in' power for evangelism. Consider this story from South Africa from Bishop Peter Lee of the diocese of Christ the King, near Johannesburg.

'Some years ago when I was serving as rector of St Luke's, Orchards, a young man came to the evening service and asked one of our clergy how he could become a Christian. When questioned about how he came to be there, he said: "I'm a jogger. I run past this church every Sunday morning when the people are coming out of church, and I can see in them and their relationships something which I don't see anywhere else, and I want it."

'To top off the story I should add that we were in the middle of a series of six fierce expositions of the book of the Prophet Amos, and had certainly not been doing a "come to Jesus" kind of evening.'
Mike McCoy, from Good News People, CPSA.

INVITING PEOPLE TO WORSHIP

In 1986 Berta, wife of the Bishop of Lebombo, Dinis Sengulane, wanted to make her apartment more attractive, so she went to buy some pot plants. The man who sold them was an out of work gardener, so she invited him to do some work on the church garden. It emerged in conversation that he was an Anglican, though he didn't know the Bishop nor Berta. He didn't go to church, he explained, because there was no Anglican parish where he lived, in the poorer area of the Mozambique capital Maputo called Te Tres ('three Ts'). Berta suggested that they start a church in his home. At that time the diocese was running a training course in evangelism. So Berta decided to ask a woman who was involved in the course to help start the new church.

On the following Sunday they came to the gardener's house in Te Tres. His family was there, but he was nowhere to be found. So Berta and her friend did what Jesus would have done. They spoke to people in the nearby marketplace, in the streets of the neighbourhood, and in the houses round about, inviting anyone interested to the gardener's house. About 15 responded.

They did the same the week later and the number doubled. By now the gardener had confirmed that these two women were indeed Anglican, so he joined the young church that had started in his house.

Within five years the house church at Te Tres had grown to 100 members, had a full-time catechist, and was dedicated to St Bernard Mizeki. Most members had no previous church affiliation. They had come to faith by simply responding to an invitation to join a worshipping community.
Mike McCoy, Good News People, CPSA.

✛

PEOPLE NOT PROGRAMMES

Raquel is a new convert who lives with her family in a village outside Asuncion, capital of Paraguay. Like most people in that country she was brought up a Roman Catholic. Her parents, in the style of old fashioned Catholics, had forbidden her to read the Bible, and once when she was a child they burnt a copy they found her reading.

Some years later, now married and the mother of children but still a nominal Catholic, she was visited by two Jehovah's Witnesses. Being totally ignorant of the Bible she found their views fascinating and persuasive. So she invited them back to talk more. One of Raquel's neighbours, an Anglican, noticed the JWs calling at her house. Alarmed, she hurried over to warn Raquel about the teachings of this sect.

That was the beginning of Raquel's journey to fullness of faith. With the encouragement of her neighbour she joined the local Anglican congregation, and soon her family followed her.
Mike McCoy, from Good News People, CPSA.

✛

AN OPPORTUNITY FOR SOUTH-TO-SOUTH PARTNERSHIP?

Asians from the Indian Sub-Continent came by the thousands to East

The Story

Africa at the turn of the century as labourers on the railways. In time they became very good business people and they have a crucial role in the economies of Kenya, Tanzania and Uganda. None of them were Christians. And to this day, because cultural differences stand in the way of Africans evangelising them, most East African Indians have never been reached with the Gospel.

'If the Christian community from India could send pastors and evangelists to East Africa, I'm sure it would be a great step forward,' says Bishop David Gitari from Kenya. 'It's very difficult for Africans to evangelise Indians because they keep to themselves. But maybe if people from India were to bring them the Good News, it might be a different story.'

Every-member prayer partnership
The Church in Trinidad and Tobago, in the West Indies, has a practice of encouraging its people to say a standard prayer at noon every day. As well as boosting committing in the Church, it is often the starting point for evangelism with fellow workers or other people who church members may happen to be with. The whole diocese is thus in partnership in mission.

South to North Partnership
Last year, as part of the celebration of the 500th anniversary of Christopher Columbus's voyage, the Church in the Southern Cone of South America sent a team of 13 to spend six weeks doing evangelistic work in Spain. Their hosts were the Spanish Reformed Episcopal Church which is part of the Anglican Communion.

'They went to two centres which were highly secularised and where there were no Protestant churches,' explains Bishop Colin Bazley, Primate of the Southern Cone. 'One of the first things they had to learn was that there was a culture gap between them and the local people, even though they spoke the same language. The Church in Spain rented a shop building on a corner site. It was covered with graffiti. It was dirty and dark inside. They took it over, painted it right through and then began their outreach. They did street work, using mime, sketchboard preaching, and a lot of children's work with nearly 400 kids. At the end of eight weeks they left behind a group of 35-40 adults who are meeting each week for worship, a children's work and work among women. Now the Spanish Church has written back to us and asked us to send back to Spain two of the members of the team for a period of two years. It means that we are moving into a new phase in the life of the Church in South America. Up till now "mission" has been something done to us. We've never sent people before like that. So it's an exciting stage for the Church to be at.'

Take up your cross
The Diocese of Chichester, England, is encouraging church people to wear a specially-made lapel cross as a conversation-starter. People who wear it are given a supply of cards explaining the Christian faith.

+

THE VISION GOES INTO ACTION

I am returning home from a parish visitation. The phone rings in my car. It is Marie Elizabeth, my wife. 'Donnie is dying. He is in the General Hospital. He wants to have Holy Communion with you before he dies.' I head to the hospital. My heart remembers the friendship Donnie and I have had since I confirmed him. We found him in the street, abandoned because he had AIDS.

I enter the hospital room to discover 13 or 14 of the strangest looking people. Muscle men, tattooed motorcycle gang types, their girl friends.

Bishop Dyer at the final press conference

The Story

With my purple shirt I look strange to them. On his death bed Donnie was conducting an Addicts Anonymous meeting.

His dying months had been spent evangelising drug addicts, alcoholics, bringing them to Christ and a drug free life. At the time of his death he had nine groups going. What a collection of strangely beautiful people were there to celebrate his life at his funeral! They all prayed:

> The Lord is my shepherd
> I shall not fear
> Though I walk through the valley
> of death
> I shall fear no evil
> for you, O God, are with me!

A transforming vision: suffering and glory in God's world.
Bishop Mark Dyer, USA.

✝

CHRIST GOES BEHIND BARS

Just about everyone has heard of Thailand's policy of handing down massive sentences, as much as 100 years with no release, to people caught smuggling drugs. For over six years Canon Monty Morris, vicar of Christ Church Bangkok, has been visiting some of the prisons where these people, most of them very young, are kept. But amid the dross there are signs of hope. Canon Morris reports: 'For quite some time, after being inside the women's prison for three hours every month to take communion, I was overcome by a tremendous feeling of guilt whenever it came time to leave. At times like these I found the girls beginning to minister to me, as they assured me they would be alright until my next visit and to "Go on home". So a wonderful relationship has developed. In six years, only five girls have left for home. A life sentence is a long time. On the Christmas visit a year ago, the girls announced they had a surprise gift for me.

'The surprise was an announcement. Two months previously, they had formed their own church, their own permanent worshipping congregation. They had been given permission to meet every Sunday for worship, as well as my communion visit on one Saturday a month. They had not told me about it before, "in case it was a flop". These girls are realists.

'Their church has blossomed. There is now a branch in the Klong Prem men's prison nearby. There are over 30 babies in the women's prison, mostly children of Thai mothers. Christ Church Behind Bars monitors their

needs, tells us what to buy, and distributes medicine, clothing, and toiletry items for use inside the prison.'
From the Mekong Messenger

ONCE FOR ALL?

If the Church is to communicate the Gospel in a way that takes root it must take people's world views seriously. The point is brought home in this modern missionary story told to me by Bishop Paul Richardson whose diocese is in the New Guinea highlands.

'Central to the world view of the Chimbu people is the concept of reciprocity. Relationships are initiated, deepened and sustained by the exchange of gifts. No expression for "thank you" exists in their language: favours must always be returned in kind. When the first missionaries arrived in the 1950s, they put the Cross and justification at the centre of their preaching. They emphasised how much God had done for the Chimbu people by dying to take away their sins, and that Jesus' death sealed their salvation "once for all".'

Converts flooded into the church. Land was readily donated to the mission and church buildings, and schools were quickly built as the Chimbu hastened to pay Christ back for what he had done for them.

However, a time came when enthusiasm flagged. The Chimbu came to feel they had done enough to reciprocate what Christ had done for them on Calvary. 'Mipela i bekim pinis' (We have paid him back) was what they said.

What the missionaries had failed to realise was the need to present the gospel in such a way that the Chimbu saw their relationship with God through Christ as a continuing reality in their lives. Lutheran anxiety to stress the once-for-all nature of salvation as a free gift of grace got in the way of effective evangelism.

'Interestingly, a missionary anthropologist from a conservative evangelical mission first identified the problem and compared the original approach with that adopted later by the Catholics who because they saw salvation as an on-going process, never allowed the Chimbu to think they had paid off Christ for his benefits.'

+

THE GREAT COVER-UP

Sometimes where one culture imposes itself on another, events come full circle. Mrs Faga Matalavea from West Samoa (Aotearoa, New Zealand and Polynesia) shared a pair of posters from her part of the world making the

The Story

The Great Cover Up!

point. A century ago missionaries to the South Pacific ordered the local people to adopt Western-style clothing. Now that is the order given by local people to scantily-dressed Western tourists!

'TOTAL' MISSION

Reaching the vast, drought ridden, remote and sparsely populated Marsabit region of Kenya, home to the Turkana, Gabbara, Borans and Sambura tribes, has prompted the Church in Kenya to do mission in its totality.

'We are combining a whole range of development, medical and educational activities as well as evangelism,' explains Anglican Bishop David Gitari. 'The Turkana migrated to the southern part of the region about 40 years ago. Until 1980 we did not have any work there. It was then I sent one clergyman. On the first Sunday he managed to get about nine together, and they worshipped for the first time. It was the first-ever Anglican service in Isiol area. From that humble beginning this clergyman started penetrating the Turkana community. Before the end of the year the number had increased to 100 worshippers.

'In about 1985 or so we got seven acres of land and that became the base of our work. We began a programme aimed at increasing food production. It included demonstrating how to raise chickens and rabbits, and how to grow drought resistant crops. It included teaching people who had been nomadic to grow crops like beans and maize. Then because they herd animals we started a programme to help them take better care of them. We showed them how to keep their cows and goats free of lice and other insect pests. We introduced vetinary programmes. Water was scarce. Women used to have to walk miles and miles to bring back water. We sunk bores in strategic centres. In time they became centres for our work. They become just like an oasis. As time went on we were able to tell them that we were doing all this for the sake of Jesus Christ. There was community conversion. They started building small churches all over the area.

'One day I remember going to one church and baptizing 257 people: the whole community. Another day we baptized 180. We needed about 20 priests to assist. Since there was not much water, we had to sprinkle them very lightly!

'Most of the women wanted to be baptized "Martha". There were so many that after a while the priests decided they would have to think up different names for them on the spot. So they went down the line of Marthas saying "I baptize you . . . Mary . . . Lydia . . . Naomi." So there has been a wonderful combination of development and evangelism. The whole community has been transformed.

'I still have one problem. The people grow food, but the elephants keep coming and carrying it off. Every town I visit the people say, "Bishop, you have taught us so much. But can you teach us what to do about those elephants?" '

+

USA

A Conference of the Decade of Evangelism leaders of ECUSA held last November/December drew over 240 persons lay and clergy, from Alaska to Panama, and from all ethnic and racial groups. Visitors included three representatives from the Church of Canada and one from the Church of England. They met in the snowy but beautiful heights of Glorieta in New Mexico, for five days of intensive learning and envisioning for the Mission of the Church.

Presiding Bishop Edmond Browning of ECUSA

There were signs of hope and renewed zeal for evangelism combined with a desire to learn from one another. They were aware of the need to develop programmes for lay training and to involve the laity in evangelism and the mission of the Church. Also the need for an emphasis on spirituality, reality in prayer and knowing the power of the Holy Spirit in evangelism and living out their Christian Faith. There was an intense awareness that the power to transform society comes from a life transformed by the Holy Spirit.

+

CANADA

From the beginning of this decade the Anglican Church of Canada identified participation in the Decade of Evangelism to be a high priority for the life of the Church. Both the clergy and laity from each diocese formed the Primate's Evangelism Network to share initiatives and resources. The Church is launching out in several directions – lay training through the 'Seminary without walls' – special outreach to 'native' Indians – plans to launch out in vigorous outreach and reforms as an expression of their commitment to the 'Decade of the Church's in Solidarity with Women' as an important corollary to the vision of the Decade of Evangelism.

+

MELANESIA

The Melanesian Church reports of rich harvest as the people launch into the Decade. With their characteristic vigour and enthusiasm they have launched out with retreats and training for clergy and laity, leading on to rebuilding community, outreach and holistic ministry led, in most cases, by the Melanesian Brotherhood.

+

ENGLAND

A large congregation gathered in St Paul's Cathedral, London on 23 September, 1992, to witness the launch of Springboard, a training initiative of the Archbishops of Canterbury and York, which will help unlock the potential of congregations and dioceses throughout the country for evangelism. Springboard is being headed up by Canon Michael Green and Bishop Michael Marshall. It has been agreed that the 'two Michaels' will be avail-

The Story

able to spend up to two months each year in training and evangelistic work in other Provinces of the Anglican Communion.
Bishop Michael Marshall and Canon Michael Green

+

WALES

The weather didn't stop the 3,000 Welsh Anglicans from marching through the streets of Cardiff, singing and praising God, to celebrate the Festival of Praise ('Spirit 2000'), in July 1992. Months of preparation for this festive day, of sharing their faith and giving witness to the Gospel in their lives, had involved teams visiting dioceses and parishes throughout the country. Teaching and training the 'know hows' of witnessing and participation in various kinds of evangelism as well as learning songs, the combination of which brought renewed life to many parishes. To quote their report, 'When we set out on this venture we were sure of only one thing, that we felt led by the Holy Spirit to run a youth service in the middle of Cardiff. We are committed to the task of evangelism. We learnt that if evangelism is to work then it must begin in our own hearts as we constantly turn to the Lord and return to him.'

+

GHANA

The Anglican Diocese of Kumasi officially launched the Decade of Evangelism in a colourful reaffirmation Service on Sunday, 31 May 1992, at the Cathedral Church of St Cyprian's the Martyr. Attended by over 1,500 men, women and children, The Rt Revd Edmond Yeboah, the Bishop of Kumasi, led the congregation to commitment to the mandate of the 'Decade'.

On 28 May 1992, 3,000 church members walked through the principal streets of Kumasi carrying banners, wearing T-shirts imprinted with the Diocesan crest and an evangelistic message 'Preach the Word', dancing to the music from three brass bands. The dancers were not only the youth but also the older men and women, the clergy and the bishop, and were very prominent in the launching of the Decade of Evangelism.

Prior to this, a three-day open air crusade, attended by over 2,000 people, was organised by the Diocesan Director of Evangelism, the Revd Canon R.K. Koomson. Many surrendered their lives to Christ.

Special prayer rallies focusing on the 'Decade' were held in many parishes. Seminars on evangelism, Bible studies, different aspects of evangelism, sharing of experiences, worship and prayer were part of the preparation for the event.

+

NIGERIA

The Anglican Communion's largest Province, with over nine million members, has continued to take the lead in mission and evangelism in Africa's most populous nation. Nigeria's nine missionary bishops, consecrated in 1991 to launch the Decade of Evangelism, are making outstanding impact through the power of the Holy Spirit as they lead youth and laity in mission and evangelism in various parts of North and Southern Eastern Nigeria.

+

SINGAPORE

The Diocese of Singapore together with Sabah began the Decade of Evangelism with an 'Anglican Congress on World Evangelism' attended by over 800 Anglicans from 40 nations including bishops, clergy and laity. The Congress was over a period of six days involving seminars on evangelism, practical training sessions and participating in an evangelism outreach. This resulted in a sense of purpose and renewal for both clergy and laity who streamed out into other dioceses around the world as invitations came to share their experience in order that others may learn. The Diocese is emphasising outreach into high-rise apartments which is giving exciting results. Their church planting programme, already effective in Singapore, is now penetrating into Indonesia, Thailand, Vietnam, Cambodia and Laos. In preparation for this their Diocesan Mission Convention 1993 will focus on the six countries of the Diocese.

+

FIJI

A week-long lay conference on evangelism was held in September 1992 attended by around 1000 participants. The Diocese produced a well-planned programme for the training of the laity in evangelism and basic doctrines of faith and practical Christian living, several Hindus turning to Christ through extended family contacts and through prayer and healing ministry and friendship evangelism. Ethnic differences are swallowed up in enthusiasm for a common concern for Gospel outreach.

As related by Dr Cyril Okorocha

The Story

✝

Running the Family

When the Early Church met in Council it brought people from a whole variety of cultures and backgrounds together in one place. They ate communal meals. They worshipped and prayed. They debated endlessly. Unlike those of us brought up on Parliamentary procedures and under the constraints of airline timetables, they were never content to decide issues by a vote. Theirs was the way of consensus: 'It seemed good to the Holy Spirit and to us.'

The first-ever Joint Meeting of the Primates of the Anglican Communion and the Anglican Consultative Council had a formidable task. As well as being confronted with a challenging agenda it was an experiment, bringing these two bodies of consultation in the life of the Anglican Communion under a single roof. As far as the agenda is concerned, it is surprising just how often consensus prevailed. As for the form of the meeting, the debate continues.

For the Primates, their meeting is a rare opportunity for peers to unwind together and talk frankly about issues, without the glare of publicity. At Cape Town some were concerned that the format of the joint meeting squeezed this precious time together too much. There was concern, too, that the Primates might have an undue influence on the thinking and work of members of the ACC.

The ACC, which brings together bishops, clergy and lay people, has been labelled 'the workhorse of the Anglican Communion', attending to the nuts and bolts of its on-going life. Most of those present at Cape Town would willingly concede the first point, and for their part members of the ACC had no strong feeling of being overshadowed. The question remains, however, whether the Anglican Communion can afford to have these two bodies meeting separately? What would have been the message to the wider Church, for example on ecclesial community, if the ACC had met and given its viewpoint, and then a few months later the Primates had met and said something even marginally different? All that strengthens the suggestion that in future these two bodies should meet in one place, though not always as a single body.

For over a decade and a half there have been differing schools of thought as to whether the traditional pattern of three consultative bodies: the Lambeth Conference, Primates' meetings and the Anglican Consultative Council should remain. The definition of the Primates' meeting and its role is clear. Some question the Lambeth Conference because of its unwieldiness and cost, preferring a strengthened ACC.

Running the Family

The Archbishop of Cape Town and the Archbishop of Canterbury at Malmesbury

THE ACC

The debate about the ACC and its composition came under close scrutiny at Cape Town. For example, if Joint Meetings are to be the future pattern, with the Primate of each Province always a 'given', will discussion be properly balanced, particularly as regards lay representation? Lay people

The Story

were certainly in the minority at Cape Town, though they were hardly a silent minority.

The Running the Family working group brought forward a revised model for representation in the ACC, assuming continuation of some form of Joint Meeting:

Group 1: Provinces with over one million members: one bishop, one priest and one lay person.

Group 2: Provinces with between 250,000 and one million members: one bishop or priest, and a lay person.

Group 3: Provinces with less that 250,000 members: one lay person.

With eight Provinces coming into the category Group 1, this would yield eight bishops, eight clergy and eight lay persons. With 12 Provinces in Group 2, this would yield 12 bishops or priests, plus 12 lay persons. Group 3, with 15 Provinces, would provide 15 lay persons.

Totals: 28 bishops and clergy; 35 lay people, in total 63. Under this arrangement the bishop on the ACC should not be the Primate of the Province. Add to that the Archbishop of Canterbury and six co-opted persons (including two youth) this would bring the total to 70.

This suggestion will be considered further by the Joint Standing Committees of the Primates and ACC. Before it could be finally adopted it will need to go before the General Synods of the Member Churches with two-thirds voting in favour.

+

The next Lambeth?

It is for the Archbishop of Canterbury to decide about things like Lambeth Conferences, and he customarily invites the bishops who attend. Cape Town was an opportunity for Dr Carey to hear a variety of views on it.

For the African bishops Lambeth is the high-point of their career and for them it would be unthinkable to scrap it. As the Ugandan bishops under Amin found, those living under pressure in their home countries can use it to enlist world-wide support.

The problem is that Lambeth is becoming an expensive, mammoth operation. By AD 2000 the number of Anglican dioceses will have risen to about 800. Can a meaningful Conference be held with such large numbers? Such a Conference would be expensive. The cost of running a three week event is likely to be in the region of £4 million.

For the Primus of Scotland, the Most Revd Dick Holloway, 'The present-style Lambeth Conference has become too big to be meaningful, and must be scaled down,' he said. But how? Diocesans only? That would mean that Suffragans of huge areas such as West Ham in East London, England, would not get a ticket, while a diocese with 30 parishes would.

Some clergy and laity at Cape Town wanted to see an equal investment in their work. Tim Goodes, a youth representative from Australia, made this point. 'Why is it that we can raise vast amounts of money for something like a Lambeth, yet we can't fund essential ongoing work.' This point was re-echoed by the Revd Barbara Clay of Canada. 'If we can spend £4 million on a Lambeth Conference and yet we do not spend on essential network work, we are going to hear from our clergy and laity via their chequebooks.'

Dr Muriel Porter (Australia) said she had initially been sceptical of the value of Lambeth. But listening to the bishops present she had been convinced of its value. 'Have your Lambeth,' she said. 'But be very prudent about the kind of Lambeth, and its costs.'

The Archbishop of Canterbury made it clear where he stood in principle. 'We are an Episcopal Church. If we were to lose this pillar it would put great pressure on our Anglican Communion.' But he was more than aware of the problem that spending £4 million on another Lambeth posed. He accepted the rightness of what clergy and lay members had said and added, 'We may come to a point of asking if it is moral for us to be spending that sort of money on ourselves.'

+

Table Talk

Getting procedures right wasn't easy in a meeting of so many cultures and languages. Early on Archbishop Michael Peers of Canada, who was in the chair, asked delegates to put up their hands if English was not their first language. Half the number put them up. The clamour is getting stronger for more translation of documents. There are many competing pressures on the Inter-Anglican budget, but in future the Secretariat will have little choice but to arrange translation into several key languages.

One relatively successful innovation at Cape Town was that except for working groups, delegates sat in permanent groups around round tables. Putting people of the same language groups on the same table with translators helped. Bible study discussions took place here. And it was possible even during plenaries for members to confer with their neighbours and that took away a lot of the potential heat when procedures got bogged down.

Most would have agreed with Archbishop Desmond Tutu who once said 'Anglicans are lovable and untidy.' The bit about being lovable certainly

The Story

stood the test of two weeks. But at times members wished proceedings were just a bit more tidy.

INCLUSIVE LANGUAGE

ACC 7 at Singapore asked that wherever possible inclusive language should be used, in particular during worship and in official documents. At Cape Town the issue surfaced again, with some delegates critical of some of the selection of hymns used during worship. The meeting asked the Joint Standing Committee to ensure that as much as possible, all future documents, presentations, and acts of worship should use gender inclusive language.

FINANCE

On the last day of the Joint Meeting, members were given a list of all the resolutions passed and asked to vote for them in priority order. This simple strategy reflected one of the most prominent sub-texts to emerge during the two weeks. There has been a shortfall in contributions by member Churches to the Inter-Anglican budget. It first came to light at the last ACC meeting in Wales and has grown since then from £80,000 to just over £200,000.

There are two main factors responsible:

- Without exception every Church throughout the Communion has been hit by the world-wide recession; and
- The combination of inflation in England and shifts in currency exchange rates have taken their toll, with member Churches being asked to pay their contribution in UK currency.

Several major contributors, including Australia, United States, England, Canada and Southern Africa, have had to reduce their funding.

All this has led to a change in philosophy by the Finance Committee, which up to this meeting was chaired by the former Scottish Primus, Bishop Ted Luscombe. Now the budget is framed on the basis of 'finding out what we can do with what we have'. In addition there is a 'wish list', projects which have the endorsement of the joint meeting, but will need to look beyond the core budget to outside groups for their support. There was initial discussion on how various tasks presently undertaken in the London office could be undertaken in other parts of the world, saving costs and enabling more participation by Member Churches.

The Joint Meeting approved the budget for 1994-5 (see Resolution 57). In addition it asked Member Churches to make the budget shortfall a matter of prayerful concern, and to do all in their power to meet their quotas.

THE SECRETARY GENERAL

Canon Sam Van Culin, who has served as Secretary General since 1983, retires at the end of 1994. The Cape Town meeting was therefore his last major Inter-Anglican meeting. At the conclusion of the conference members presented him with a painting by the South African artist Stanley Hermans.

An Appointments Committee, which had already ready received 18 nominations, met during the fortnight. Some new names were added, and the list will remain open until April. Those nominated will be asked to send in a formal application. A shortlist will then be prepared, interviews held, and the Appointments Committee will put forward a nomination to the next Joint Standing Committee.

+

The United Nations Observer

1993 has been declared to be the Year of Indigenous Peoples by the United Nations. In countries like Canada, Australia, New Zealand, Latin America and the US, the Anglican Church numbers indigenous peoples among its members and there are also large numbers in the Church of North India, all of which makes it appropriate that the Anglican Communion now has an official representative at the UN who is himself partly descended from the indigenous Maori people of New Zealand. He is Bishop Sir Paul Reeves, formerly the primate and more latterly the Governor General of New Zealand.

Sir Paul Reeves is the first official Anglican representative at the UN. Despite only a very small staff and slender resources, Sir Paul is energetically pursuing priority issues identified by the Anglican Communion.

He classifies these issues under three headings: (1) indigenous peoples; (2) human rights; (3) environmental concerns. In Sir Paul's opinion, the UN has not devoted the same energy to promoting the Year of Indigenous Peoples as it has to other special years. He thinks that a number of governments feel threatened by land claims and the demand for autonomy on the part of many indigenous peoples.

The Story

The meeting with President de Klerk

Sir Paul has been personally involved in human rights issues. He recently made an intervention on human rights before a UN Commission on behalf of the people of East Timor. Another recent task was to take up the cause of the Episcopal Church in Iran, whose property was confiscated during the country's revolution.

One of the environmental issues that Sir Paul's office is carefully monitoring is the question of toxic waste disposal, in particular the effects on the peoples of the South Pacific. Lady Reeves has a special brief for family issues and care for the aged.

✢

The new Province of Korea

On 16 April 1993, the Province of Korea will become the thirtieth self-governing Province of the Anglican Communion. The Archbishop of Canterbury, who has been Metropolitan of the three Korean dioceses, will be present for the inaugural celebrations. Anglicanism came to Korea in 1880. Today there are 81 parishes, led by over 100 clergy. Recent years have seen significant growth. One of the key projects agreed by the new Province is development of its theological college, based in Seoul. Its aims include the exploration of the Korean Christian identity, including indigenisation and contextualisation, and to work on the Korean Church's ecumenical task.

+

The Crying Mother

Sudan is one of the largest countries on the continent of Africa. After four decades of almost constant civil war, the land is often referred to as 'The Crying Mother' who weeps for her lost children. There has been a tragic flow of Sudanese blood as, under different regimes, those who do not belong to the ruling class or follow the State Religion are denied basic human rights.

The situation in the Sudan tends to be overshadowed by events such as the civil wars in Ethiopia, Somalia, Angola, and most recently Yugoslavia. As a result the international community has paid little attention to the sufferings of its people. With few prospects for peace the suffering of the people increases every day. The Anglican Church in the Sudan is appealing desperately to the international community to recognise the plight of the Christian minority who suffer in this continuing war.

Despite the toll of death and famine of recent years the Anglican population is estimated at about one million. Nine out of 10 Anglicans live in the south of the country. The rest are scattered in pockets, while a small number live around the capital Khartoum.

Anglicans have been hard hit during the four decades of war. Family life has been disrupted, with cultural values shattered and destroyed. Many have been forced to seek refuge in neighbouring countries, while others have left their homes to shelter around the besieged towns of the south. Recently division within the Church which resulted in schism and the consecration of a number of rival bishops has been healed.

'Help us tell the world about our need', pleads Provincial Secretary, the Revd Nelson Nyumbe. 'Come over to this Macedonia and help us.'

+

Reconciliation in Rwanda

A great service of reconciliation was held in a stadium in the capital, Kigali, in June 1993. The service celebrated the healing of deep divisions which had developed in the House of Bishops which threatened schism in the young Church, and was the prelude to the inauguration of French-speaking Rwanda as a separate Province in the Anglican Communion.

The Story

'Now our main concern is to strengthen our new-found unity: in our Church and among her leaders. Visitations to dioceses, conferences for priests and their wives, and organising evangelistic meetings are all steps to accomplish this purpose,' says Provincial Secretary Bishop Jonathan Ruhumuliza.

+

Living in sin

It's called 'shacking up', 'living together', 'co-habiting' or even more pointedly 'living in sin'. For hundreds of years unmarried men and women have lived together as though they were married. But for a variety of reasons this is on the increase in the modern world. Hardly any culture is exempt. It is certainly widespread in Western nations such as the UK and USA.

The problem of what to do about it pastorally prompted the Archbishop of the Indian Ocean to raise the issue at the Cape Town meeting. In his Province, 'eight out of 10 children are born out of wedlock. It's becoming culturally accepted because it's so common, even though there is a stigma and guilt deep down,' he said.

These relationships take two forms, he believes. There are couples in a casual relationship, which doesn't last. Then there are couples with no intention of being legally married, though 'they fulfil the requirements of marriage as best they can. They are faithful to each other and bring up their children, sometimes better than the children of married couples.'

For Canon Monty Morris, rural dean of Thailand and the Mekong, there is a serious pastoral problem on how the Church should respond to the 400,000 Burmese refugees in Thailand who are not permitted under Thai law to marry. 'Tens of thousands of couples are co-habiting. What are these couples going to do?'

'I'm looking for information from around the Anglican Communion about the extent of the problem and how other Provinces are dealing with it,' Archbishop Chang-Him said. In his country the Roman Catholic Church, the predominant Christian grouping, tried to discourage the practice by baptizing children born out of wedlock on Fridays instead of Sundays. But this didn't work. 'This raises the whole question of what is marriage,' he said. It has implications, too, as far as the sacraments are concerned. Traditionally co-habiting couples automatically 'excommunicate themselves'. But should the Church make a distinction here between 'faithful concupiscence' where it is a faithful life-long relationship and casual relationships?

✝
Communication . . . fast

Canon Sam Van Culin pressed a button on a computer. Within seconds his message had been transmitted simultaneously to 30 overseas destinations. The message was just five words: 'We are on line'. The Inter-Anglican Information Network, IAIN for short, was born.

The Inter-Anglican Information Network, first operated in 1984, makes use of the most economic means available to enable communication among leaders and members of the world-wide Anglican Communion. It helps co-ordinate the delivery of messages and documents through fax networks, computer networks and regional or Provincial networks. It is now using the Quest International computer network, available now in over 60 countries, was endorsed by the 1988 Lambeth Conference and again by a Plenary resolution at Cape Town. The introduction of Quest makes exchange of information quicker and more economical than ever before, even when great distances are involved.

IAIN had staff members as part of the Communications Team at Cape

IAIN demonstration at the University of the Western Cape

The Story

Town, offering daily information sessions which 20 Provinces attended. Those involved were the Revd W Clement Lee (USA), Cliff Hicks (Australia), and Stewart Ting Chong (CPSA). The principal programme funding for IAIN is provided by Trinity Church, New York, which has also provided seed money to help Provinces and dioceses introduce and use telecommunications.

+

New ways of working

New technology and a desire to give a different shape to the way the Anglican Communion tackles its ecumenical agenda has prompted the Anglican Communion Office to experiment by re-locating its ecumenical officer in Canada.

Canadian-born Dr Donald Anderson will set up office at his home in Toronto. He still plans to spend up to 16 weeks alongside staff in London. He believes the plan has at least four things to offer the Anglican Communion:

- it will be cheaper, both for the Inter-Anglican Budget and for himself personally;
- it will be an opportunity to explore how an international organisation can work with a dispersed staff;
- it will enable closer links with the Canadian and US Churches and thereby create new possibilities for ecumenical work as a result;
- it will open up new approaches to the whole ecumenical agenda.

Welcoming the move the Secretary General Canon Sam Van Culin said: 'An international office doesn't have to be located in one geographical centre anymore. The laws and taxes are against this anyway. It's a case of being open to the future and with Paul Gibson we have already tested this.'

+

Post Script

One of the great delights in being part of the Cape Town meeting was enjoying the company of our host, Archbishop Desmond Mpilo Tutu and his wife Leah. Most of us will remember him for his laugh.

Perhaps his vintage performance was at the Good Hope Centre on the first Sunday of meetings. Introducing a long vote of thanks, he told the con-

Post Script

gregation that the first thank you should be to God. 'Let's give him a standing ovation,' he suggested. When the din subsided a huge smile broke across his face. 'I once did that in Australia. When it was over I said 'Thank you".'

Yet those who witness his humour are sometimes apt to underestimate both his spiritual power and his unyielding opposition to the oppression of his people. He told how he once put a friendly Nationalist politician in his place after the man had claimed to be his Member of Parliament. The

At a township: Mrs Eileen Carey greets the children along with the Archbishops.

The Story

Archbishop pointed out that since he didn't have a vote he couldn't have a Member of Parliament.

The same sharp wit came through in one of the more untidy business sessions when he somehow managed to vote the wrong way over safeguards for those opposed to the ordination of women. When laughter pealed out he smiled: 'You see, we are not used to voting in South Africa.' He said the presence of so many brothers and sisters from throughout the Anglican Communion had been a 'shot in the arm' for his Church.

His country faces difficult times in the future. But he is adamant that God has given his people a great gift, which will be crucial in seeing them through. It is the gift of forgiveness. 'It is very difficult but I think God has given us a gift. You look at Namibia, you see there Sam Nujoma who was regarded as an ogre by the whites. Now he is seen as the laughing father of the whole nation. In Zimbabwe Ian Smith is allowed to be a Member of Parliament. Yes, we hurt and agonise and there are wounds but you can't spend time brooding. You've got to move on to try and build a new future, a new South Africa. You can't build it on anger, resentments and hatreds. As long as those who have wronged have the capacity to say "we're sorry", then we forgive and dust ourselves off and say "off we go". We have a tremendous country for all of us, black and white, and it's going to be even more tremendous for the sake of the sub-continent and maybe for the whole continent.'

Recently the CPSA agreed to release him for a task of peacemaking and reconciliation in his community. As a Christian leader he stands above party politics. 'I will be just as critical of today's oppressed if they become tomorrow's oppressor,' he has said.

We will be praying for him and his Church all the way.

John Martin is Editor of the Church of England Newspaper

The Plenary Presentations

Communion and Commission

The Rt Revd Michael Nazir-Ali,
General Secretary, Church Missionary Society

Before I speak to my subject I would like to pay tribute to the Revd Prof. David Bosch who was a noted missiologist in South Africa and who was very courageous in his Christian witness against apartheid. He tragically was killed last year in a car crash very soon after publishing his magnum opus, *Transforming Mission*, which I am delighted to see is on sale here. I shall refer to David's work in the course of my address, I need to thank my colleagues who led yesterday on the 'Dynamics of Communion', because they brought out quite clearly the connection between Communion and Mission and this is going to be the burden of what I have to say this morning. My talk is in two parts; the first you may want to call 'Patterns of Partnership' and the second you may want to call 'Modes of Mission'.

Patterns of Partnership

I want to begin by trying out a statement on you: 'The churches of the Anglican Communion are churches of the Reformation.' Now of course it is true that the Anglican Reformers insisted on the continuity of the Anglican Church with the medieval and the early Church. The famous Archbishop Matthew Parker even insisted on going beyond the Mission of Augustine to discerning a continuity with the Celtic tradition of Christianity, and his work on the antiquity of the Church in Britain (note not England) was an attempt to discern this continuity. So there was this consciousness of continuity; nevertheless, the Anglican Church at the time of the Reformation was manifestly a church of the Reformation and it shared many of the characteristics of the other churches of the Reformation. And one of them was an almost complete lack of a sense of mission. Now this is quite remarkable but it is almost universal in the churches of the Reformation, barring the Anabaptist tradition, and stands, of course in sharp contrast to the great missionary efforts of the Counter Reformation in the Roman Catholic Church. There are several reasons given for this lack of a sense of mission in the churches of the Reformation.

There is, for example, a geographical point that is often made, which is that the seas at that time, the sea routes, were controlled by either the

The Plenary Presentations

Muslims or the Roman Catholic powers and so it is said the churches of the Reformation had no opportunity to engage in world mission. Again, sometimes it is said that the relationship that many of the churches of the Reformation had with a particular people, a particular ethnic group, or a particular political dispensation, a state for example, precluded interest beyond their doorstep or their shores. And of course the Reformers themselves gave theological reasons for not engaging in mission; there was a curious kind of dispensationalism that was in operation and it was often said that the great commission had been given only to the Apostles and that it did not apply in other ages.

But I'm glad to say that there were exceptions to the rule and one such exception was Adrian Saravia, who was a Dutchman and who became convinced of the necessity of Episcopacy for the unity of the Church and so he became an Anglican, there being no Old Catholics at that time of course! He came to hold high office in the Church of England. Saravia fought against general apathy towards mission at that time in the churches of the Reformation and particularly in the Church of England. One of the points that he made was that the promise of continuing communion with the risen Lord which occurs at the end of St Matthew's Gospel, where Jesus promises his disciples that he will be with them until the end of the age, goes hand in hand with the Great Commission, with going into all the world, preaching the Gospel to all nations and baptizing them in the name of the Father and of the Son and of the Holy Spirit. In other words, from the very beginning, communion and commission have gone together and indeed we see that the writings that witness to the earliest period of the Church tell us that it was communion or fellowship with the Lord and among Christians that attracted people to the Gospel, to the risen Christ as proclaimed by his disciples in fellowship together. This is already apparent in the second chapter of the Acts of the Apostles, for example.

Some reference has already been made to the Epistle of Paul to the Philippians and I too would like to draw your attention to that Epistle; it is a very important work as far as mission is concerned. We find at the very beginning of this Epistle that St Paul identifies the church at Philippi as sharing with him in the partnership of the Gospel. *Koinonia eis to evangelion*: Fellowship for the sake of the Gospel. We could almost say, 'for the purpose of spreading the Gospel'. They are partners (*sunkoinonoi*) with him in the defence (*apologia*) and confirmation (*bebaiosis*) of the Gospel, they are partners with Paul. And so we find that *koinonia* (communion, fellowship) comes out strongly in terms of the mission of the church and not only in terms of fellowship among believers. In the Acts of the Apostles and in the Pauline Epistles there seem to be different kinds of partnership in mission. First of all there is the inner circle of those whom Paul calls his fellow workers (*sunergoi*). There are numerous references in the New Testament to such people, but the most important are to be found right at the end of the Epistle to the Romans, in different parts of the Epistle to the Philippians and in 1 Thessalonians the inner circle of those who engage in mission with Paul, who went with him on his missionary journeys perhaps, or who helped him in particular localities when he arrived there and, of course, among this number there are women as well as men, slaves as well as free people.

Then the second kind of partnership that we can discern is the special partnership, and once again the word koinonia is used in Philippians in the fourth chapter, with a supporting church, such as the one at Philippi. In other words, Paul and his companions look to support from particular local churches in the fulfilment of their world-wide mission. You will remember that Paul said at the end of the Epistle to the Philippians that this church was the only one at a particular stage in his career that had partnership with him, all the others having turned away. He refers to the partnership as a 'giving and receiving'. so already at that early stage this is clear. And then, finally, there is the partnership between churches which Paul is seeking to build up. There is a long argument about this in the second Epistle to the Corinthians and two whole chapters are given to the development of this argument, chapters 8 and 9. Paul is arguing that just as the churches in Macedonia, and the church at Philippi was the chief among them, of course, just as these churches had forged a partnership with the churches in Judaea, so also the church in Corinth needs to forge a partnership with the Jewish Christians in Palestine. This partnership is based on the self-emptying love of Jesus Christ, who though he was rich, yet for our sakes, became poor. The churches should give not only out of their plenty but out of their want, and he praises the Macedonian churches in particular for giving out of their poverty. He goes on to argue that this partnership is for the sake of equality. Equality is not a fashionable word these days, but that is the word that Paul uses.

Now if I may comment: the mutual responsibility and inter-dependence processes that began in the Anglican Communion with the Congress in Toronto and which were later developed by the ACC in Dublin, set in train the Partners-in-Mission (PIM) movement, for instance. These processes have emphasised this last aspect of partnership in mission, that is to say, the partnership between churches, and this has been a very great blessing to the Anglican Communion and if this is the only thing the Anglican Consultative Council will ever achieve, it is enough! But it does not fully take into account the other kinds of partnership that we find in the New Testament: the enabling and support of individuals and voluntary bodies within the church where there is a specific vocation for mission. Having developed partnership between churches so well, I think it is now time that the Anglican Communion should give some attention to these other kinds of partnership.

It is in this connection that I want to return to the work of David Bosch. He reminds us in his book *Transforming Mission* of the distinction between missionary and missionising. The whole Church is missionary by its very nature and all Christians are called to commend the Gospel by their style of life, to give an account of the hope that is in them. Once again that word *apologia* is used here in 1 Pet. 3.15, and to welcome outsiders into their midst (James 2.1-7). The whole Church is missionary but, says Bosch, there are special movements of people which are missionising, fulfilling particular vocations which further God's mission in the world. All Christians should support such people, through giving and prayer, but above all by living in such a way that the Christian mission is seen as credible by outsiders. Now of course, there are many examples of such movements throughout the history of the Christian Church: think first of all of those wandering men and women in the early Church called prophets, who went from church to church bringing a particular charism, a particular ministry to each church. And what tremendous honour they were given there! They ranked, the Didache tells us, above the local Presbyter-Bishops. They could say the Eucharistic prayer extempore; well, not even the Archbishop of Canterbury can do that!

Bishop Gore, in his work on the Christian ministry, which is still important, tells us that these prophets, as well as apostolic delegates and others, were prototypes for the historic episcopate when it emerged fully into the light and Gore was well aware that this prototype contained both men and women in the movement. So there are the prophets, but then of course there is the emergence of Monasticism, about which we can say that it is the single most influential factor in the spread of the Gospel and of the church world-wide. Monasticism began in the East, in Egypt and in Syria and in what was then the Persian Empire. We find that in every Christian tradition Monasticism has been important for mission.

We know in the West how Monasticism not only helped to Christianise Europe, but also to civilise it and to save it from the ravages of the Barbarians. But in the East also, the so-called 'Nestorian' Church, the Assyrian Church of the East, engaged in significant mission, which had lasting consequences in India, China and in parts of central Asia and it was the monks who took the Gospel to these parts. The Coptic tradition has for long had a missionary concern and commitment to Africa which is natural of course, because Egypt is part of Africa and the Copts for a very long time worked and still continue to work in Ethiopia and on the Horn of Africa generally. As late as the nineteenth century the Ethiopian Copts

Communion and Commission

were engaged in mission to Muslims and to people of primal religions in that part of the world (making many of the same mistakes that the Western missionaries were making a few hundred miles further East!). So Monasticism, movements of people called by God to particular vocations, has been used wonderfully in mission. But then there are lay movements, traders from Syria who spread the Gospel and strengthened the Church in South India, or Russian Orthodox merchants spread the Gospel in the Far East.

In the Church of England itself, we see that in the eighteenth century, in the great ferment that appeared at that time, all sorts of voluntary movements of Christians emerged to fulfil particular tasks which they felt that God was calling them to do. I naturally have some knowledge of the Clapham Sect, in fact I have the arms of all the members of the Clapham Sect in my office and have to look at them every day! But the struggle for the abolition of the slave trade and later slavery itself, the struggle to improve the working conditions of men and women in Britain, to provide schools for the poor, all these were the result of voluntary movements, such as those resulting from the work of the Clapham Sect, in the Church of England in the eighteenth and nineteenth centuries. The Church Missionary Society (CMS) was also a voluntary movement of this kind and from the same kind of constituency. But before the CMS came into existence, the Society for the Propagation of the Gospel (SPG) and the Society for Promoting Christian Knowledge (SPCK) were also movements of people for spreading the Gospel in different parts of the world. In the nineteenth century, with the emergence of the Tractarian movement, we see the revival of religious communities in the Anglican communion and they were a very significant factor in so many parts of the world, including Southern Africa, in bringing the Gospel to people, in planting the Church and in creating a lasting Christian witness.

Now I want today to plead for the importance of voluntary movements in the Church for the fulfilment of the Church's mission. The partnership between the churches can be greatly assisted by people who are called to fulfil particular tasks. The whole church is missionary but people are called to fulfil particular tasks in that missionary church.

What is the role of the episcopate then in this context? I would say that the role of the episcopate in this context is recognising, enabling and directing voluntary movements in the Church, not controlling them. Recognising what is a work of God in a particular place at a particular time, enabling that work, letting a thousand flowers bloom (if it's still permissible to quote Mao Tse-Tung)! We need to think about directing people to where there is a need for the Gospel. There is a need also for balance between canonical obedience to bishops and archbishops and the freedom to take initiatives. Obedience should not repress or suppress initiative. Look at Paul and his companions; they reported regularly back to the church that sent them and yet they were able in the middle of all of that to respond to the promptings of the Holy Spirit, sometimes in quite radical ways, like taking the Gospel to Europe!

Of course, if these different patterns of partnership in mission are going to be taken seriously, they will need to be embodied in the life of the churches. And we find that this is precisely what is happening and this is very encouraging. For example, in the Church of England, we have recently taken a step which brings together the voluntary mission agencies and representatives of General Synod into fellowship with each other in a common committee which is answerable to the Church of England as a whole and which belongs to the structures of the Church of England. Such a structure now needs to be reflected in discussion and parochial life and, perhaps in the life of General Synod itself.

Some years ago I was invited by the Episcopal Church in the USA to a consultation that they held to consider how their unit for World Mission could relate to the many voluntary movements that were coming into being in the Episcopal Church. As a result of that consultation, I believe, they arrived at some kind of arrangement which facilitates dialogue between the two sides. In Tanzania, the Anglican Evangelistic Association has a particular relationship with the province. The Mar Thoma Syrian Church, a church with which we are in full communion, has its Evangelistic Association which has carried out pioneering missionary work in Nepal and Tibet and many other parts of the world. The Church of South India, a united church in full communion, has the Indian Missionary Society which they support.

At the last meeting of MISAG – the Mission Issue Strategy and Advisory Group – (and by the last meeting I mean the very last, because there aren't going to be any more MISAG meetings), a recommendation was made that there should be a standing commission on mission in the Anglican Communion and that this commission, which we provisionally named Missio, should have within it representatives from provinces in the 'North' and the 'South' and representatives from mission agencies and other voluntary movements in the 'North' and the 'South', because we found that in many 'Southern' contexts too God was raising up people to fulfil particular tasks and we wished to encourage this.

Now one of the questions you might want to ask yourselves is: 'what patterns of partnership are appropriate for your church, your province or your diocese? And how are these patterns incarnated in the life of the church at congregational, diocesan and provincial levels?'

Modes of Mission

Coming now to Modes of Mission first of all, there is roaming. You remember the 'go' of the Great Commission, 'go into all the world...' Now this 'go' is usually read as an imperative: 'you should go', 'you have to go', etc., but my reading of the text suggests that it needn't be because it could be translated 'having gone...disciple all nations' (Matt. 28.19). In the early Church people often found themselves in a place not because they had gone there intentionally but because they had been displaced by harassment or persecution (e.g. Acts 11.19f). Such displacements have always been significant for mission. It is certainly true that more and more people are finding themselves in a particular place not intentionally, but because that is the way it has happened. We need to consider here the significance of the displacement of people, the large-scale displacement of people in today's world. There are refugees in so many different parts of the world and these refugees have a particular significance, I believe, for the Church. When, as a result of the tyranny of Idi Amin, some Ugandans had to flee to Zaire, the result was a great strengthening of the Church in Zaire.

In the Sudan, there are at least seven different reasons for the displacement of peoples. And yet we find in all this displacement, and perhaps because of it, the church has grown tremendously in particular parts of that country and indeed in neighbouring countries. In other parts of the world the displacement of people has meant that the Church can now minister to people to whom it had no access in the past. Think of the Somali refugees in Northern Kenya, for example, or of the hundreds of thousands of Iranis in the cities in Australia, in Melbourne, and in Sydney, and also in New York, Los Angeles and London.

But although the displacement of people in this way is significant for mission there is also an intentional 'going', isn't there? Going back to Archbishop Parker's tracing of the continuity of the Anglican Church with the Church of the Celts we find that 'roaming' was a fundamental aspect of Celtic Christianity, it had to do with their make up. They roamed, of course, for different reasons, but as they roamed, they began to realise that this roaming was significant for mission and gradually the roaming became intentional as far as mission is concerned, and so we have the great stories of the evangelisation of Northern Britain by people like Columba, of the missionary work of Columbanus in continental Europe, of Aidan and Chad and of the establishment of Iona and Lindisfarne as centres of mission. We have to be prepared to go with the Gospel, ready to meet Christ when we arrive. The roaming of the Celtic saints was not aimless, it was

The Rt Revd Michael Nazir-Ali during his plenary address at the University of the Western Cape

not hit and run, they established important centres for the nurture of those they evangelised. It was directed and committed.

So 'roaming' then leads to remaining – to the establishment of Holy Island and to the nurture of people who would take over leadership in the churches which had been established. And if roaming is the Celtic paradigm, remaining is the Augustinian one. Gregory's charge to Augustine, when he was sent out rather reluctantly to England on his mission, was to take the culture of the local people seriously, not needlessly to destroy what he found there, but somehow to transform it by the proclamation of the Gospel. And it was this charge, I believe, which is at the root of the Anglican commitment to incarnation which has been mentioned so many times already and we find that one expression of this commitment was the creation of the parochial system under Theodore of Tarsus.

But of course it is not only Anglicans or the Church in England or Britain that was and is committed to incarnation, the Franciscans on the continent of Europe, for example, had a very well-developed and sophisticated view of incarnational presence, particularly in relation to mission to Muslims. You will remember that they were among the first to advocate a peaceful approach to Islam. Their view was that at first, and sometimes for a long time afterwards, all Christians need to do is to go and live in particular place, a particular culture, among a particular people, to learn their ways, to hear their stories, to live as Christians, to minister to people's needs and to discern the right time, the *Kairos*, for the proclamation of the Gospel. Now that may take centuries or a few years, or only a few days, but they distinguish between presence and proclamation and it is still right of course to do that.

Presence should result in penetration of culture. Presence can be alienating, if, for instance, the church in a particular place represents one class interest over others; then the other classes will be alienated. I remember a priest in the Church of England who came from the East End of London saying that when he announced to his family that he had a vocation to the priesthood, he was regarded as a traitor, because this was seen as class treachery! Choices in terms of liturgy, music and even the physical arrangements of a church, can attract or alienate people from the church. And so presence needs to be more than presence, it needs to come to grips with the world view, the beliefs and the values of the people where the church is present. It has to identify as well as to be present and in this connection we find that the first Inter-Anglican Theological and Doctrinal Commission that was chaired by Archbishop Keith Rayner did some valuable work when it pointed out that although the Anglican Reformers regarded reason as a universal human faculty, that was the same in every culture and among every people, in fact we now know this is not the case.

Every culture has its world view, its values and its beliefs and it is the glory of the Gospel that it can appeal to the world view, the beliefs and the values of each culture. It is these that constitute the 'reason' of every culture and the Gospel has to find 'hooks' into this reason. I find this re-interpretation of reason in the Anglican triad of scripture, tradition and reason very attractive indeed. Now, of course, this is not just wishful thinking; as a matter of fact, during the course of history this is precisely what has happened: the Gospel has actually appealed to many diverse world views, values and beliefs. And so we find that we reach a stage when the Gospel so permeates a culture, influences it, so materially, if you like, that a whole people can call themselves Christian. National or popular churches, in other words, come into being. Armenia was the first nation to call itself Christian and there was a Christendom in Ethiopia before there was a Christendom in Western Europe. Then there are the Georgians, the Copts and so many others whose cultures were so permeated with the Gospel that national churches came into existence.

Now of course a church can be national without being established. The Roman Catholic Church in France, for example, is clearly the national church of France but it is certainly not, at least since the revolution, established. And then there might be different kinds of establishment: the Church of Scotland is established, but the nature of its establishment is rather different from the establishment of the Church of England. If establishment is seen as a desire by the people of a nation to give a place to the Church in the decision making structures of the state, it may be acceptable. Such an arrangement would also allow the organs of state to have some say in the affairs of the Church. But this should not compromise the Gospel nor result in a weakening of the Church as the body of Christ where believers are strengthened for mission. Of course, the Church should not be a sect and should be open to people of all kinds, committed and uncommitted. The Church should also be open to advice and criticism from all sides. But that does not mean that the uncommitted and the casual visitor should have a determinative say in the affairs of the Church. If that begins to happen then we are going in the direction of compromise and in the loss of a sense of purpose. Archbishop Michael Ramsey rightly believed that the Church must have control over its own doctrine and worship (and one might add appointments) while remaining open to the participation in its councils of people drawn from across the spectrum of national life. Such people should be able to influence but not to determine the church's priorities in the fulfilment of its task.

Now while the Gospel has an attachment point (*anknupfungspunkt*) [that is a word that Emil Brunner used] with every culture, a proper estimate of the doctrine of the Fall also leads us to the view that the Gospel, not the Church, judges aspects of cultures, their world views and customs. This

Communion and Commission

critical principle is found already in the capacity of the Old Testament Prophets to oppose corruption, oppression and idolatry in contemporary Israelite culture, including of course its religious aspect. This is why I say that it must be the Gospel, the word of God, and not the Church that judges. We find that this prophetic work is continued in the ministry of Jesus and in the life of the early Church, in the opposition to emperor worship, for example. Charles Elliot who used to work for Christian Aid relates the contemporary Christian concern regarding structural injustice and social sin to the rediscovery of the centrality of themes such as justice and mercy in the biblical witness. And of course I don't need to underline that in South Africa this prophetic ministry of the Church has been recognised by international and national leadership. But there are examples from other parts of the Anglican communion, such as East Africa where the Church was the first to speak out against an unjust government.

In liberation theology from South America, this prophetic witness is brought to bear on the Church as well as the world, as the Church is seen as implicated in the oppression. The popular, the prophetic and the witness then of the persecuted church: we have heard about this already this morning in the Bible study from Nigeria and in the fact, that we are today honouring the memory of Yona Kanamuzeyi, who was martyred protecting the weak. Although the persecution of the Church under Marxist regimes has disappeared or is disappearing, we find that the Church is being persecuted in other parts of the world by other kinds of people, and this needs to be taken seriously by the Anglican Communion, because not only are these fellow Christians but many of them are fellow Anglicans. As I have noted in relation to the Sudan, persecution often results in great blessing for the Church. The blood of the martyrs is indeed, as Bishop David said, the seed of the Church. This witness of the persecuted church the world hears and we need to hear.

The whole of Christian mission, however it is exercised, presupposes dialogue and depends upon it. There can be no Christian mission without dialogue, as dialogue is the basis for all human community. Communities have dialogue internally: how to order themselves on questions of law and order and justice, for instance, or on matters such as the distribution of resources. Communities who have dialogue with each other about fair trade or about the need for peace. And so the Church too finds itself engaged in dialogue on a whole number of fronts. What then is the scope of the Church's dialogue? We have noted already the dialogue with cultural values and beliefs. The representative from the Democratic Party in South Africa said that the basis for his party's actions was a belief in the innate dignity of all human beings. The Church's dialogue with such belief, which is widespread, needs to ask what is the basis for this belief in the innate dignity of human beings? Here the Church may have something to say! Dialogue with the scientific community: what is the basis for that intelligibility of the world by the human which makes science itself possible? Dialogue with those in the arts: George Steiner said recently in his book, *Real Presences*, that all art is concerned with transcendence; well, if that is so, what is the Church doing about it? In fact he goes further and says that all post-war European art is concerned with only one question – the presence or the absence of God! And then there is the dialogue with people of other faiths and ideologies: Is there a common spiritual quest in which we are all engaged? If so, what is the unique Christian contribution to this?

What is the theological basis for the Church's dialogue? Now I want only to mention four points: The first, the *imago Dei*, the image of God in all human beings, which is certainly affected and spoilt by sin, but not destroyed by it. The Church can address humanity, can address human groups and cultures because of the surviving image of God in them. And then, this was mentioned in the first Bible study by the Archbishop of Canterbury, the presence of the Logos, the light of the eternal Word in all human beings that St John talks about in his prologue to the Gospel. This, of course, was picked up by some of the early Fathers, by Justin Martyr and Clement of Alexandria in particular in their idea of the *Logos Spermatikos*. They saw the work of the divine Logos especially in the philosophy of their pagan context, in the practical morality of the Stoics and even in the prophecies of the oracles. There is a foretaste of this in Paul's speech at Athens (Acts 17). And then there is the presence and work of the Holy Spirit in the world and not only in the Church, and once again the Johannine writings alert us to this, the Spirit bringing the world to a knowledge of righteousness and of sin and of judgement.

Now dialogue can be practised in a whole number of ways: there is for instance, discursive dialogue, where the parties exchange information about themselves and their beliefs. Then there is interior dialogue, where people talk about their spiritual experiences and each attempts to understand the other's. There is also dialogue for the building up of a community in which the different sides live and dialogue about the recognition for our common humanity. Today, there is much dialogue about how the different faiths view the environment and how we can gain insights about the right relationship with our environment from the different traditions. There is also the dialogue which makes common study of a particular issue or belief with a view to removing misunderstandings and clarifying matters. Some people say that dialogue is all very well, but it is not enough and these are the protagonists for direct action. They have had their supporters throughout Christian history; the ransoming of slaves, the visiting of those in prison, going to the disreputable parts of the cities in the ancient world to minister to the poor, the long-term educational and medical commitment of the churches and today the provision of relief and longer-term community-based development and service to the poor all depend on such 'activist' views. But there are some who say even that is not enough; these are the people who argue for direct action, in terms of participation in social struggle to secure justice in society, and some World Council of Churches programmes have taken this on board. The Programme to Combat Racism (PCR) and the Commission on the Churches Participation in Development (CCPD) are actually based on the philosophy of such direct action, where community is to be found with the poor, solidarity with the poor, to take their side in the conflict which must precede the securing of justice for them, in their conscientisation which enables them to organise and in their liberation which enables them to be co-creators of their own future. Co-creators, of course, with God.

As we engage in different kinds of mission and in different ways, we find that we come to a point where we need to declare the Good News of Jesus Christ. In fact, as we engage in mission in its different ways, we find that declaration is an aspect of each of these ways. It is not an accident that *Kerysso* and *Kerygma* are related words in the Bible. In other words, the meaning of the Gospel is disclosed in its proclamation! We are called to challenge people through word and act and attitude to consider the claims of Christ, to invite them to follow him and to nurture them in the Faith. But of course this is a subject which the Archbishop of Canterbury will address this afternoon. I leave a question with you: what are the most effective ways of 'translating' the Gospel into your culture? Are there any limits to inculturation? What are they?

BIBLIOGRAPHY

1. David Bosch, *Transforming Mission*, Orbis, NY, 1992.
2. See further Paul Avis, *Anglicanism and the Christian Church*, T. & T. Clark, Edinburgh, 1989, pp. 24ff and V. J. K. Brook, *Archbishop Parker*, Oxford 1962, pp. 322ff.
3. Michael Nazir-Ali, *From Everywhere to Everywhere: a World View of Christian Mission*, Collins, London, 1990, pp. 38ff, G. Warneck, Protestant Missions, Edinburgh, 1906, pp. 8-9.
4. *Partners in Mission*: Dublin 1973, SPCK, London, 1973, pp. 53ff.
5. op. cit, pp. 137ff.
6. Charles Gore, *The Ministry of the Christian Church*, Rivingtons, London, 1889.

The Plenary Presentations

7. Nazir-Ali, op. cit, pp. 22ff.
8. J. D. Davies, *The Faith Abroad*, Blackwells, Oxford, 1983.
9. *Towards Dynamic Mission:Renewing the Church for Mission.* The Final Report, MISAG II, ACC London, 1992, pp. 49ff.
10. J. Bulloch, *The Life of the Celtic Church*, Edinburgh, 1963.
11. G. R. Evans and J. R. Wright (eds.), *The Anglican Tradition*: *Handbook of Sources*, London, SPCK, 1991, pp. 78f.
12. Jean-Marie Gaudeul, *Encounters and Clashes : Islam and Christianity in History*, Rome 1984, pp. 151ff.
13. Nazir-Ali, op. cit, p. 39 and pp. 139ff.
14. *For the Sake of the Kingdom : Report of the Inter-Anglican Theological and Doctrinal Commission*, ACC, London, 1986, pp. 38ff.
15. See further Aziz Atiya, *Eastern Christianity*, London, 1968.
16. *A New Dictionary of Christian Ethics,* London, SCM, 1986, 'Economic Development', pp. 175ff.
17. Nazir-Ali, *Dialogue in an Age of Conflict.* D. Cohn-Sherbok (ed.), *Many Mansions*: *Interfaith and Religious Intolerance*, London, Bellew, 1992, pp. 72ff. See also George Steiner, *Real Presences* , CUP, 1987, and John Polkinghorne, *One World : Interaction of Science and Theology,* London, SPCK, 1986.
18. See Eric J. Sharpe, *The Goals of Inter-Religious Dialogue* J. Hick (ed.), *Truth and Dialogue*, London, Sheldon, 1974, pp. 77f. Also *The Challenge of the Scriptures:The Bible and the Qu'ran*, Muslim-Christian Research Group, Orbis, New York, 1989.
19. John Paul II, *Redemptoris Missio*, London, CTS, 1991 pp. 36ff.

Mission and Evangelism

The Most Revd George Carey, Archbishop of Canterbury

Lord, inform our minds and inflame our hearts with love for you in the name of Christ our Lord, Amen.

I'm grateful as you will be to Michael Nazir-Ali for his splendid contribution this morning. We are grateful for the theological thinking that he's doing for us in the Anglican Communion and in this he continues the fine Church Missionary Society tradition of reflection and action combined in mission and evangelism. I see my session and Bishop Michael's session as a kind of wallpaper for the working group on Evangelism. My role today is rather like the Lord Mayor of London's dustman's cart which follows behind the November procession sweeping up what the Lord Mayor has left behind, so I'm coming trundling along behind Michael Nazir-Ali.

One of my favourite stories is of a little West Indian boy, back home in Jamaica, standing by a quayside watching a cargo ship load up casks of molasses, and as he's looking up watching with longing eyes, suddenly one cask breaks open above his head and the little boy is drenched from top to bottom in this thick, treacly substance and not the least bit deterred he's heard to say, 'Lord give me a tongue worthy of the task!' The reason why I share the story with you is because there is a second 'E' word we need to take on board for the task of mission. 'Enthusiasm'! Nothing is ever done without it. Enthusiasm, if you like, is the other side of love and what you love, you speak about. What you love you never tire of talking about; what you love you will communicate, but enthusiasm and love on their own are insufficient, we need to know what we are talking about, what the issues are, what are the challenges before us and no two situations are alike. What I want us to do is to reflect on some of the challenges facing the modern church, and the issues that confront us.

The first handout is designed to draw out some of these issues; paragraph 1 points out that Evangelism never stands on its own as if it's distinct from Mission. My God is an evangelising, loving God who reaches out into his creation. The *missio Dei* – the mission of God – is the total activity of God in renewing, in shaping, in regenerating. Jerry Falwell's statement, that our only purpose on earth is to know Christ and make him known, is a dangerous half-truth. If that were the whole truth then

MACRO   **MICRO**

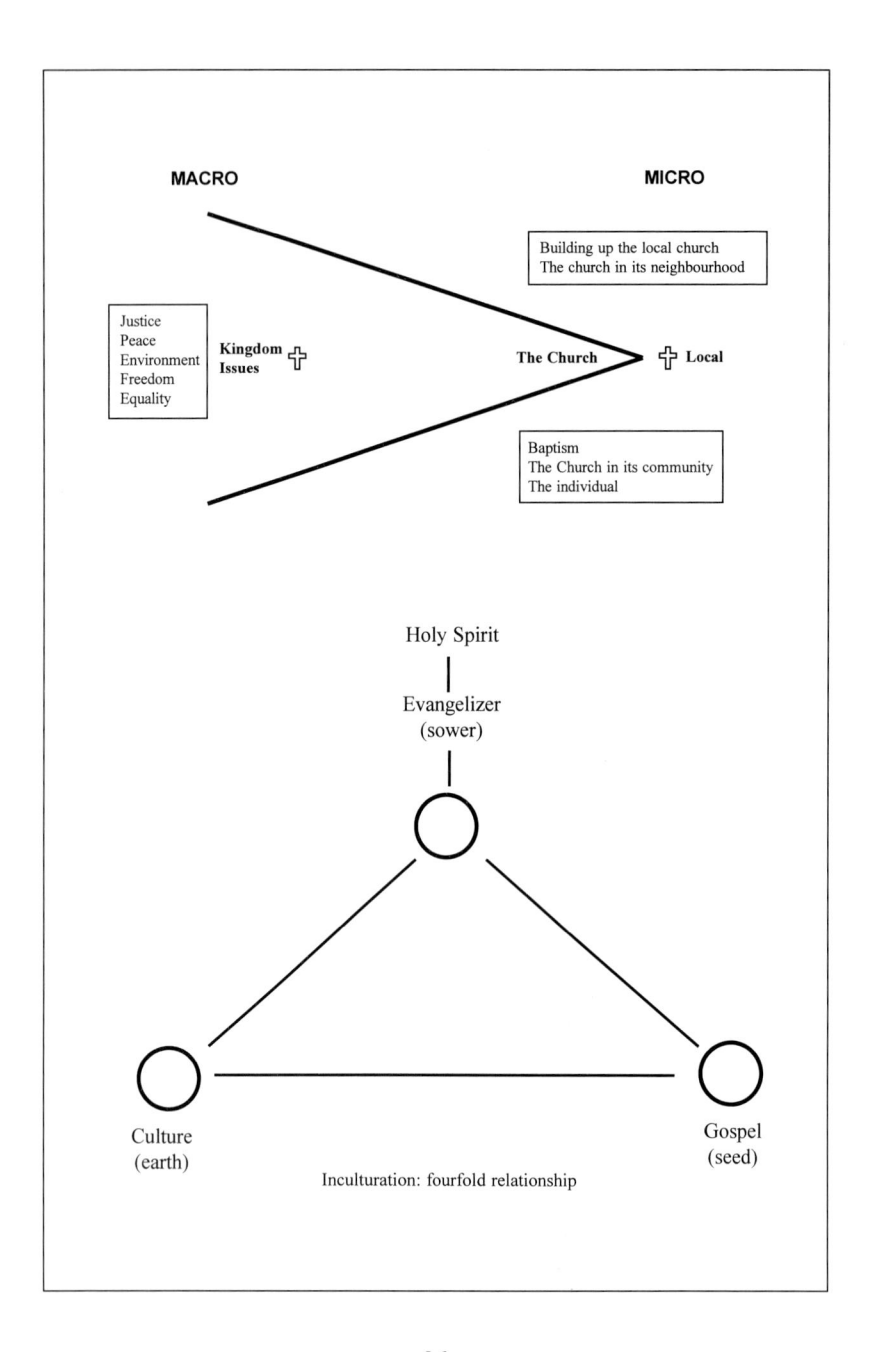

Building up the local church
The church in its neighbourhood

Justice
Peace
Environment
Freedom
Equality

Kingdom Issues ✝   **The Church**   ✝ **Local**

Baptism
The Church in its community
The individual

Holy Spirit
|
Evangelizer
(sower)

Culture
(earth)

Gospel
(seed)

Inculturation: fourfold relationship

Mission and Evangelism

Archbishop Desmond Tutu has been wilfully wasting his time here; he should not have got involved in the social and political activities of South Africa. I want to assert that, on the contrary, what Archbishop Desmond and the church here have done, is directly related to the Gospel and Evangelism. Christ didn't simply come to preach words at people. He healed them, he challenged the order of his day, he challenged ways of looking at people, he touched the lives of the unprivileged, women, slaves, children. And while it is true that the Church exists to proclaim Jesus Christ as Lord and Saviour, it doesn't do that in isolation from its ministry of compassionate care. It enters into the saving activity of God as it engages holistically with the cares of life.

You would have noticed in the video (*The E Word*, Anglican Church of Canada) the great difficulty that people had in defining Evangelism. They included words like: loving, sharing, inviting, belonging, being with, accepting. We then move to the context in which our Evangelism takes place. Paragraph 2 is a reminder to take culture seriously. Wasn't it Goering, the Nazi leader, who said, 'When I hear the word culture I reach for my revolver'? He saw culture as a threat to Nazi imperialism. And culture is a threat to us all because we have to enter into the strangeness of others.

It's only very recently that we Christians have discovered the importance of culture or that word 'inculturation'. A lot of missionaries in the last century went about quite oblivious of the need to contextualise their work. Robert Gray, the first bishop of Cape Town, went around here with the Book of Common Prayer, with the Authorised Version, with his Englishness. Quite innocently he foisted that upon the church, almost an innocent oppression, which accompanied Evangelism. We need to understand our culture if we are going to make connections for the Gospel. Of course there have been some very enlightened people in the past. My namesake, William Carey, a Baptist missionary who lived 200 years ago, was a very remarkable man. He spent something like 14 years understanding Hinduism before he felt it appropriate to speak about Christ in a Hindu culture. And Panikkar's book, *The Hidden Christ in Hinduism*, controversial as it may be, must be seen as a serious attempt to connect culturally with Hinduism. Of course culture may be harmless, but it may also be demonic.

When the first missionaries went to India, there were things in Hindu culture that they could gladly accept, and as bridges into understanding. But there were other things that they couldn't accept, they had to preach against. Among the things that the early missionaries saw in early Hinduism were the abandonment of children, the immolation of wives on the funeral pyres of their husbands, the caste system itself, those things had

The Plenary Presentations

to be directly challenged. In paragraph 3, we are introduced to three important words and the first word is the key word, 'inculturation'. It's that dynamic process between the Christian message and the culture we are seeking to address. It's an on-going critical interaction and assimilation both ways. In my visit last year, to Papua New Guinea, I saw something of the way in which our church there has taken over many of the customs and made it possible for the Gospel to travel into the culture. Inculturation is that interaction between Gospel and Society. In my country, and maybe this is true of your country too, it is quite false to talk about English culture. There isn't such a thing as English culture, there are dozens of cultures in my country and we have to recognise that variegated element. This has liturgical implications which Bishop Colin James touched upon. The working-class culture from which I came really finds middle-class culture quite difficult as an expression of faith. This may be true of your situation as well.

The word 'inculturation' is much more of a process by which we are assimilated into our culture. We are all children of our culture. I've imbibed Englishness from my earliest years and I've therefore acquired a fine set of prejudices which have little to do with my Christianity and that is true of you as well. All of us have to learn to survive in our society because we find we can only survive by conforming to it. But as the Gospel penetrates our lives more and more we begin to question that formation. We start to examine our prejudices: what is our justification for considering ourselves better than another person? We tease out the relationship between the two. The third word, 'acculturation', is more sinister. It's the unconscious transfer of customs and cultural forms which belong to dominate society.

I want to commend to you a very remarkable book, which Bishop Paul Richardson brought to my attention in Papua New Guinea last year, *Earthing the Gospel* by Gerald Arbuckle. It's called an 'inculturation handbook for pastoral workers' and it's as relevant for the first world as it is for the third world, in fact relevant to all our situations. Among many an example of acculturation there I picked out the time in the fourth century when Christianity became the religion of the Roman Empire. Suddenly the oppressed Church of Jesus Christ became the privileged church of Constantine. Bishops became people of power overnight.

Churches, once the refuge of the poor and the weak and the victimised, became the place of the wealthy and the honoured. Churches became popular – beware when Christianity becomes popular – and without consciously realising it, gradually the churches became carriers of Imperial power, a form of acculturation.

Paragraph 4 is concerned with urbanisation. Some of you might think

Mission and Evangelism

that this is only a problem for economically well-developed countries: this is not so. As the population expands, the Church is challenged to respond in appropriate ways to the needs of people and in paragraph 4 I give the example of Bishop Blomfield, Bishop of London in the last century. He was a very good bishop and what he tried to do, and did, was to build 200 churches because he thought that by providing the churches people would automatically go to them. They didn't and they still don't. He failed to realise that church buildings presuppose communities where the Gospel has already penetrated. I think the church is still searching for appropriate ways of Evangelism in urban areas.

Paragraph 5 takes us into a problem confronting many churches. The term used these days is the word post-modern, a rather arrogant term used in referring to the shaking of the foundations going on today scientifically and philosophically. The hard facts of materialism, the hard facts of science itself are being deeply challenged by new science, by quantum physics. Post-modernism is a peculiar term given to the new world in which we live, a world of uncertainty about the meaning of science itself, not as hard and as immutable as once thought. Poor religion, instead of dying out, has actually proved to be the victor of Communism and Nazism. There is no secular ideology around these days. Are you aware that since the beginning of this century Christianity has trebled and Islam has quadrupled? Unfortunately the growth hasn't been even, but even in the hard, hard West and the harder Europe no one in his or her right mind would ever talk about religion dying out. What kind of religion are we talking about?

The dominance of religion is not actually good news. Religion itself needs converting. Religion can dehumanise when it's intolerant or fundamentalistic. In one of our London papers last week, I read that in a certain African country where a different religion prevails five women who were caught in the act of adultery were stoned to death. And as I read that into my mind flashed John, Chapter 8, where Jesus said to a number of people, who were about to stone a woman caught in the act of adultery, 'Let the person without sin cast the first stone'. Religion, I want to suggest, is perhaps the greatest challenge to Christianity today. It takes two forms, a challenge to our Christian religion because we find demonic forms of that within our own faith. One of my own predecessors, Archibald Tait in the last century, actually was attacked very bitterly because he had subscribed money to the Salvation Army. He remarked that 'The greatest evil is that liberals are deficient in religion and the religious are deficient in liberality.' I find some English clergy apparently more interested in the right forms of the liturgy than they are in the Gospel itself. The challenge is not only about religion itself, but also religion around us, other faiths. The good news is that people still need God, the bad news is that there is no simple solution to

Bishop Edmund Yeboah, with Bible raised, leads a congregation in an oath to the principles of the mandate for the Decade of Evangelism

Mission and Evangelism

how we communicate that good news to other people. The 'E' word is not an easy word and I'm rather glad it isn't, because human nature does not come ready-made like a factory product. We are unique creatures with those precious qualities which cannot be cribbed, cabined or confined.

Before I move on into a more practical section, I want you to see a bit more of the Canadian video. What we see now are a number of television adverts that the Anglican Church in Canada produced.

Trying to get a simple message across conveying something about the life of a community is something you may want to discuss, a little later on. What I want to do is to build on what I have said and talk about the dynamics of evangelism, in the second hand-out. This begins with the primary data of our faith. We are not in the business of keeping the rumour of God alive. I'm not interested in rumours – I don't know about you – but I'm interested in promoting a full-blooded Christian faith which is rooted in an historic faith, open to new truth from whichever direction it comes. And so our faith is trinitarian, is biblical, is credal and is Anglican. What is the character of Anglican Evangelism or Evangelisation? Does it have a definite shape? I think it has and I want to suggest a six-fold shape to you.

First, it is incarnational. Paragraph 2 of the second hand-out related that just as our Lord took human form and was born in a certain place, at a certain time, in a certain culture, so true Evangelism is rooted, it is incarnational; it has an incarnational presence, as Bishop Michael said. He referred to Archbishop Theodore who created the pastoral or parochial network in England. You will think immediately of many illustrations from your experience of the incarnational shape. I can think of my own. I was born in the East End of London and my parents, although unchurched, were very influenced by the Anglo-Catholic priests of the East End, whose ministry was deeply incarnational going out from strong church centres, loving and caring for the poor. So a church must begin where it is, rooted in community, knowing its community by being identified with its problems, getting to know the children, the old people, the middle-aged, the businesses in the community.

When I was a vicar in Durham, many years ago, it was my aim to plant the Christian faith in the community to make sure that Christians were among the political and social leaders of the community. I tried to get the Church out of the building into the place where people live. I believe an Anglican faith is incarnational; also it is deeply pastoral. Have you noted at the end of John's Gospel when Peter is recommissioned again, Jesus didn't say to him, 'Peter I want you to go out and evangelise'? What did he say? He said, 'Feed my sheep, feed my little ones, tend the flock.' In North London there used to be a store which had the motto, 'We grow by caring' I believe that could be said about many a church which is growing. Look at its pastoral care. Is it showing the love of God in action?

The Plenary Presentations

Then there's the third identification of Anglican Evangelism in the word 'sacramental'. A sacramental church believes that the Gospel touches the lives of people at all points of their living. I want to give an illustration that made a deep impression on me. Bishop John Taylor, formerly Bishop of Winchester, told me a lovely story about a mistake he made which he is quite prepared to share. He had a young gardener called Tom. Tom and his wife very rarely went to church. Then Tom one day came up to the bishop and said, 'Bishop, would you baptize our first-born child?' and the bishop was glad to do so. On the given Sunday they went along to the church and it was a wonderful baptism service with a working-class family; there was laughter ringing around the church and it was a glad occasion. The baptism went very splendidly.

As Bishop John and his wife left the church with the family John's wife said, 'John, have they invited us to tea?' and John said, 'No, no one mentioned that to me.' So the family went in one direction home and the bishop and his wife went back to their palace. The following day Tom said to the bishop, 'Bishop, did I offend you yesterday? I'm not used to church words. Did I make a mistake in what I said? You know we were terribly grieved that you didn't come home. Why didn't you come and have tea with us? It meant so much to us and we didn't really have a party without you being there.' And John said to me, 'I suddenly realised that I didn't hear a liturgy that was being sung that day.' He went on to explain that there were many liturgies going on, being sung around us, liturgies of happiness, liturgies of bereavement and sadness, liturgies that take us right in the heart of a culture and he failed to pick up a liturgy being celebrated that very day. I believe that goes to the heart of the weakness of the church very often, busy singing its own liturgies, failing to hear the songs of celebration and sadness going around us. So by sacramental, I don't only mean the sacrament, of course that's important, because the sacraments of baptism, eucharist, penance, confirmation, whatever you define by a sacrament are ways in which people open their lives to God, but all the other points of contact which Jack Martos talks about: the doors of the sacred, ways in which God can be known. Now how can we build on that?

Incarnational, pastoral and sacramental mission

We Anglicans take spirituality seriously, at least we ought to. We have traditions of spirituality, too, which overlap with Roman Catholicism. We have religious orders; their presence is in this very hall and active throughout this province. We have forms of prayer, we believe in spiritual direc-

Mission and Evangelism

tion, and all this is part and parcel of our religious life. This is also part and parcel of our evangelism as well. How can this be nurtured? How can this be shaped? When I tell you that 70 per cent of English people actually pray to God and probably only 10 per cent go to church, you will realise that there are levels of spirituality going on in the lives of people that we as church people have not yet touched. How can we tap that?

Last year I took 1,000 young Anglicans to Taizé and it was a marvellous experience for me. I don't know exactly what it did to them, but many of these youngsters learned more about prayer. And as they learned more about prayer, their hearts were warmed with the love of God. Many of them, I'm sure, in the days to come will feel a call to ordination. Many more of them will feel a call to share their faith with others. But knowing God takes another form. This is not only the formation which comes from spirituality, but the informing, the information, which comes from knowing about our faith. I have to say that we Anglicans are not actually very well-informed Christians and I believe we've got to do much more work together on knowing our faith, helping young people to understand their faith, understanding the basic shape of apologetics, because what is central to Anglicanism is our emphasis upon reason.

We do believe the Christian faith is a rational, reasonable faith. It's rational to be a Christian. It's not irrational, it's believable, but we need to help people to understand the framework of the Bible. We need to help them to understand the questions that modern Christians have to wrestle with.

The next thing to mention is an appropriate catechism. I came into the Christian faith in my late 'teens and when my vicar prepared me for confirmation, he took me through the catechism in the Prayer Book. I think we've lost the catechism. I mentioned in my notes that we actually can learn a great deal from Roman Catholicism in terms of the right to a Christian initiation. I believe that that process is a very thorough one and maybe the Anglican Communion needs to do much more work on initiation forms in order to prepare people for baptism, in order to nourish the formation. If there is such a thing as Anglican evangelism, it is incarnational, it is sacramental, it is pastoral, it is spiritual, it is catechumenal, it is intelligent. Those six points – how do we put them into practice?

In paragraph 7, we see that the Church must begin to live on the outside of itself. What is the sign of a dying church? It's when the organism is replaced by organisation, it's when survival becomes our overwhelming concern. Look at the budget of any church organisation, see what it spends on mission, on young people, on young adults, on Sunday schools, on the wider community, and compare that to what it spends on itself. Then you will get a measure of whether it is growing or declining or standing still or

The Plenary Presentations

just simply interested in maintaining its own life. I believe, as the MISAG document suggests, that we must be prepared to look critically at our structures, at our bureaucracy, to see who we really are serving. Are we serving the kingdom of God or ourselves?

If this is to be a challenge to our churches, what message do we want to send out from here, from the ACC, from the Primates' Meeting? I hope that identifying the challenge will come from the working group back into our plenary sessions. We must establish relevant plans, we must plan for growth, we mustn't settle for a comfortable existence. Leaders must challenge and lead the people of God forward. We must be less clerical. The emphasis on ministry has its downside because by emphasising the ordination of women and the priesthood we can actually isolate our lay people from the ministry and mission of the church. The development of lay life, the affirmation of lay ministry, the equipping of lay people, the readiness to involve lay people at every level of church life, must be among our priorities. Without raising the issue of the ordination of women to the priesthood again, let me just simply remark that we still haven't found ways to use the creativity and gifts of women in the leadership of our churches. We have still yet to see the full potential of women in the church. Worship has to be revitalised, and it doesn't mean to say we remove all the old forms, but that we seriously look critically at the cultural implications of our worship.

Finally, I must say something about mission in an inter-faith context (paragraph 8). I've already said that religion is not dying out. It's increasing, in fact, and the presence of other faiths around us and among us has changed the nature of Christian evangelism. It's no longer possible for us to present our faith as if there is no other faith in sight and although that doesn't mean that we have to apologise for it, it does require us noting the areas of overlap. The overlap is important because we may begin to see what we can do together with people of other faiths. Hans Kung's book on global ethics has a great deal to teach us there. We have a mission to people of other faiths as well as to all people.

The christological dimension of our faith is crucial; in fact, it's definite, it's definitive and it's decisive. We are told to go into the world and preach the Gospel, and some of you are doing that in areas where Islam is strong and vibrant. You have much to share with us. Some of you are doing that in places where Buddhism or Hinduism or Sikhism are powerful; how do we evangelise in places like that? The answers are many and complex, but I find in situations like that that Christianity comes across as very talkative and very complicated and very complex. Do you remember those words in E. M. Forster's wonderful book, *A Passage to India*, in which he mentions poor little talkative Christianity, and we talk and talk and talk, and make the whole thing so complicated, that we compare unfavourably with the simplicity of other faiths. How do we compare that and our methods with the uncomplicated way in which Jesus Christ addressed people by attractive narrative, by parable, by drawing people closer in to the Christian faith?

In conclusion evangelism is not simple; it is complex, variegated, and there's not one single method. We are called to explain it as attractively and simply as we possibly can. Evangelism is the church in action. We must talk less about it and do more about it and put it into practice. Evangelism begins with leadership, you and me and what are we going to do about it. Evangelism means establishing goals and what does that mean for the Anglican Consultative Council? The MISAG document suggests some possibilities and one of them is the possibility of a mid-term consultation in 1996.

Let me, finally, share one dream with you. I have a dream of a renewed Anglicanism, a renewed Anglican Communion reaching out in service, living in glad obedience to the Lord of the Church, contemptuous of survival but expectant that the Christ who calls us to go into all the world is the one who will keep us until his kingdom comes. I'm a devotee of the Scottish poet Edwin Muir, and in one of his poems he talks about a new church being built in New England but he doesn't know what denomination it is. It could be Orthodox or Catholic or Anglican or Protestant, but as he sees this new building going up his soul is stirred by it and his poem ends in this way:

> *Yet fortune to the new church*
> *and may its door never be shut*
> *or yawn in empty state to daunt*
> *the poor in spirit, the always poor.*
> *Catholic, Orthodox, Protestant,*
> *may it wait here for its true state.*
> *All still to do:*
> *roof, window, wall are bare.*
> *I look and do not doubt*
> *that He is there.*

I suggest it could be applied with a great deal of profit to your church to my church and to our communion.

May we strive for a renewal of our structures and life so that we look out into the world with all its opportunities and carry on rejoicingly with the call to go into the world and preach by life and by lip and behaviour the Gospel of Jesus Christ our Lord. Amen.

Towards a Renewed Vision of Evangelical-Episcopal Catholic Christian Church

John S. Pobee,
World Council of Churches

Let me begin by drawing attention to the word 'Towards' in the title I have chosen. I wish it to signal that even if I have a commitment to the search for a renewed vision of our communion, I also believe there can be no prefabricated vision. And certainly there is no, and will be no, and can be no philosopher-king who will hand it down to us. Together we have to search for it on the basis of our story, our beginnings, our experience and the challenges of the new times. Only a common search together will give a sustainable, and hopefully, lasting vision.

What is in a name?

It will be noticed that I have also avoided the most obvious word at a Joint Meeting of the Primates of the Anglican Communion and the Anglican Consultative Council. In a sense our story goes back to Henry VIII (1509-1547). Before him, there was a Church of England going back to Augustine of Canterbury who arrived in the Isle of Thanet in 597. Henry, by the Act of Supremacy of 1534, established *Anglicana Ecclesia*, the English church. By it he cut off the English church from the Holy See and declared himself the supreme head of the church and the English church became the church of the people (*Volkskirche*). That there was English nationalism in our beginnings may not be denied. For precisely that reason the description of our tradition becomes invidious particularly in nations which have struggled against British colonialism and imperialism. What then shall we call ourselves?

However, before we rush to scrap the name Anglican, let me say that if we were to go for another name, we may have the necessity to define ourselves by that word. And so you may change the designation to the Church of the Province of West Africa, but people have found it helpful to put Anglican in brackets to show that this creature grew out of the Anglican church. I guess I am hinting that the word Anglican is part of our history which cannot be easily blotted out. The only option is to redeem the word.

The argument, however, is more complex than that. A name is not just a label of identification; it is also a description of the identity, integrity, vocation and persona of the bearer. There is something in a name. I guess I am suggesting that whatever name we take, we should not lose sight of the fact that we are committed to the *evangel* (good news of God) and therefore to mission which seeks to share by word and deed the good news as a basis of building community of communities. And precisely that commitment to the evangel makes us Catholic, sharing with a world-wide church. We are further committed to an episcopal form of church order and are committed to be an expression of the *una sancta*, the 'one, holy Catholic and Apostolic church'.

Anglicanism, Church of England and Anglican Communion

The three expressions are related but not identical. Anglicana Ecclesia is the English church established by Henry VIII in England and is today the Province of England. It was English in culture, texture and ethos. Its language was English. Its worship and spirituality owed much to the English culture. In its development it had (from fairly early on) a Catholicising High Church tradition, as well as Protestant and Evangelical tradition, not to mention Broad Church tradition, which, so to speak, mediated between them.

However, thanks to the rise and activities of societies of a missionary nature like the Society for Promoting Christian Knowledge (1698) and Society for the Propagation of the Gospel (1701),[1] there were outgrowths in several parts of the world. And so, the Protestant Episcopal Church of the USA grew out of the Anglican Church in 1789.[2] The Church of the Province of West Africa grew out of the work of SPG and CMS.[3] What began as an English church has become a world-wide phenomenon in which more than one half of the constituency now does not have English language and culture as their first-order experience.

PROVINCES BY CONTINENTS/REGIONS

Africa: Church of the Province of Burundi, Church of the Province of Central Africa, Church of the Province of the Indian Ocean, Church of the Province of Kenya, Church of the Province of Nigeria, Church of the Province of Rwanda, Church of the Province of Southern Africa, Province of the Episcopal Church of the Sudan, Church of the Province of Tanzania, Church of the Province of Uganda, Church of the Province of West Africa,

Anglican Church of Zaire (12 provinces).

Asia: Holy Catholic Church in Japan, Church of the Province of Myanmar, Philippine Episcopal Church.

Australia and the Pacific: Anglican Church in Aotearoa, New Zealand and Polynesia, Anglican Church of Australia, Church of Melanesia, Anglican Church of Papua New Guinea.

Europe: Church of England, Church of Ireland, Episcopal Church in Scotland, Church in Wales.

North America: Anglican Church of Canada, Episcopal Church in the USA.

South America: Episcopal Church of Brazil, Anglican Church of the Southern Cone of America.

Caribbean: Church of the Province of the West Indies.

Middle East: Episcopal Church in Jerusalem and the Middle East.

Extra Provincial Dioceses: To these may be added the Extra-Provincial Dioceses of Bermuda, Pusan, Seoul, Taejon, Colombo, Kurunagala, Hong Kong, Costa Rica, Puerto Rico, Cuba, Kuching, Sabah, Singapore and West Malaysia as well as the Lusitanian Church and the Spanish Reformed Episcopal Church. It is a world-wide expression of one version of Christian religion.

It is this geographical spread that constitutes the Anglican Communion which has moved beyond the Anglo-Saxon moorings of the Church of England to embrace other cultures. It is a veritable specimen of a multi-cultural institution. It is this reality that gives us the task to search for a new vision for the Communion. The task before us is in part a quest after inter-Anglican self-definition, a family self-definition. What is the identity of this one world-wide expression of this one version of Christian religion? And that expression does not preclude particular local expressions.

Some questions

There is a whole host of questions to be addressed:
1. What is the value of the original Englishness of the Church of England in this new situation of the Communion?

The Plenary Presentations

2. Has the Communion grown out of its original Englishness to reflect and appropriate other cultures that have come into the Communion?
3. What may be deemed the Ariadne thread that runs through the Anglican tradition, whether in Ghana or England, South Africa or Canada, Myanmar or Aotearoa or the USA?
4. Is the Communion caught in Anglo-Saxon captivity? And if the answer is yes, is that detrimental to the vocation of the Communion as an ecclesia serving the purposes of God in today's world?
5. Initially, partly as a consequence of the Establishment of the Church of England, the model of the Communion was based on the model of the British Dominions/Commonwealth. With political independence and nationalism all over the world, that old model must give way to something new. What is and should be that something new? What model of a Communion is now feasible and viable? In what does the common wealth of the Communion consist?

Search for Renewed Mission

We have been in business for some 500 years. We certainly have grown in terms of numbers, breadth and, I dare add, depth. We certainly are not Peter Pan who never grows and remains a boy all the time. What does the fact of an experienced process of growth mean for our identity and integrity today? Important as our past is, we cannot uncritically be intoning or repeating it. It is not enough just to pay our dues and respects to the classical tenets of Anglicanism. More important is to explore what precisely it means today to affirm the tradition and to test the relevance for today. We have to explore on the basis of our experiences over the past hundreds of years what we could become and should be in the light of new reality of our geographical spread. So we may ask: what strength does this geographical spread give to the Communion? What energy and dynamic vision is there?

I have opted for renewed vision and not a restoration or revolution. Revolutions, properly speaking, are done without respect for received traditions. I am committed to continuity and change. I am not keen on restoration because even if there is a presumed earlier or better form, it has to be critically assessed for its relevance to the new situation. Whatever we do should foster the consolidation of what the church has and renew it in order to help the church not only to survive new developments but also to be on target as it pursues what it exists for: namely, joining in God's mission today.

I use the word 'renewed' to signal another crucial point. Renewal is possible only under the guidance of the Spirit of God. Spirituality is what will make possible the renewal of this Communion and its vision. Scholarship in the service of the search for the renewed vision of the Communion must be touched by the Spirit and spirituality. We must explore such Anglican spirituality as there is in the light of the new geographical-cultural configuration of the Communion. But it must also be sensitive to the spiritual challenges of our day. Spirituality is more than prayer and worship, important as they are; it is, as well, obedience to the will of God in bread-and-butter issues; it is, as well, vulnerability. Any church that is preoccupied with its self-preservation will die. Any church that uses mission for its self-preservation will die. Spirituality as the dynamo of our search obliges us not to be afraid to die, if the vision should lead us to that conclusion. It is a call to renewed, vibrant faith when vulnerability is pressed on us. Let me call us to a spirituality of trust. By it I signal the willingness to be vulnerable, counting on the guiding hand of the God who holds all creation in the palm of the hands. Without that spirituality, especially of trust, we cannot cohere as a Communion. A sense of our vulnerability is not only a spiritual act but also should urge us on to openness to others so that *together* we may grow and travel towards fullness of community of God's people.

Renewed Vision for the Sake of One Mission

The concern for renewed vision of the Communion is not for the sake of the Anglican Communion; it is for the sake of its obligation to be on one mission for the sake of the world. The quest is, therefore, concerned with the viability of the Communion *vis à vis* one mission today. We seek efficiency for mission in today's world and not in 1948, nor yet 1662 and earlier. But what is mission?

MISSION

Forgive me for seemingly carrying coal to Newcastle to talk about mission to Primates of a Communion that has declared a Decade of Evangelism. But like Paul said, 'to write the same things to you is not troublesome to me, and for you it is a safeguard' (Phil. 3.1). Besides, in the year in which we commemorate the 500th anniversary of the Christopher Columbus phenomenon, we need to recall that mission can become a tool of oppression, dehumanisation, etc., rather than an offer of good news. So permit me to make some basic affirmations about the mission we are obliged to do.

First, mission is a process. In an age of instant coffee and instant communication we need to remind ourselves that mission is a process. My reading of Jeremiah, especially Chapter 20, is that mission is a duty of labour, often drawn out, a burden with ups and downs, not all rosy. The question, then is what are the elements that facilitate the process? And what elements do we *together* contribute *to one another* in the Communion to facilitate the process? Notice I say *to one another* – it is not a one-way street of giver to recipient, nor yet of the old to the young. The Akan of Ghana have a saying that 'the old woman looks after the child to grow teeth and the child looks after the old woman when she has lost her teeth'. Reciprocity – a conviction that is irrespective of our circumstances – we each have something to offer and to receive as well. Forgive me when I say peoples of the industrialised North find it difficult to receive and almost consider it disabling to receive. Unless we learn to receive and to give, we cannot be in communion. What has each diocese to offer and what does it ask of others? What does each diocese need?

Second, mission is integrating proclamation, making disciples, engagement in socio-economic and political liberation 'in comprehension and dynamic wisdom'.[4] Needless to say, I find it useless to enter into debates about whether mission or evangelism is the better word. Forgive me, fathers and mothers of the church, when I dare to say that I would have preferred us to declare a Decade of Mission rather than Decade of Evangelism. For only that will measure up to the dynamism that is demanded of things relating to God who is Dunamis, Power.

Third, mission is a process of building community of communities in the one household (*oikia*) of God. That one household is not the Anglican Communion, nor any denomination, nor even the church; it is all of these and yet more. Dare we forget that Jesus said, 'there are other sheep of mine, not belonging to this fold . . . ' (John 10.16)? Are we bold enough to consider that these 'other sheep' could be African Traditionalists, Muslim, Jews or even unbelievers? But I will return to this matter of community of communities again.

Fourth, the cement for that community of communities is the values of the Kingdom: sacrificial love, truth which is never so final that it may not be revised (so far as we humans can perceive it); righteousness – justice; freedom; reconciliation and peace. Let me add that these values are at once religious – spiritual and political, economic and social. Christians do not have a monopoly on these values; we shall have to search for the content of these values in dialogue with peoples of other faiths or of no faith, with politicians, sociologists and economists. We are meeting on the continent of Africa, which bears the marks of violence – economic, political, religious – violence which is the opposite of peace. Has mission which carries the gospel of hope nothing to say alongside the UN, alongside politicians, etc?

The missionary vocation of the church should determine, inform and shape the structure of church, the structure of the Communion. What structure of Communion will be best equipped to pursue that basic aspiration and vocation of being church?

But before I proceed on that question, let me also say the church, Anglican or otherwise, should not be the primary aim of mission; rather the church is God's instrument, an instrument of God's presence, compassion and redemptive purpose – bringing all into the one household of God.

Some Contours of the Search

ANGLICAN COMMUNION AS A RELIGIOUS PHENOMENON

Professor Lewis opened his classic study of religion with the following words: 'Belief, ritual, spiritual experience; these are the three cornerstones of religion, and the greatest of them is the last'.[5] In underlining Anglicanism as a religious phenomenon, I seek to urge us to discover an identity along the lines of the three cornerstones of religion, namely spiritual experience, belief and ritual. For believers, spiritual experience has a life of its own, independent of the social framework in which it appears, even though I would affirm also that it bears the stamp of the culture and the society. I believe Anglicanism is a spiritual experience which exists independently of the social framework of the England in which it was born. Only this makes sense of the fact that a Malagash, an Englishman/woman, a Canadian, a Ghanaian and a Malay can be in the one Communion. What is that something which holds us different persons and personalities in the one and same Communion? Can we identify and describe a *residual anglicanism*, without which I or any other person ceases to be in the Communion? What is that something which distinguishes the Anglican tradition within the Catholic tradition, or any other tradition? Is there a residuum of belief that can be called Anglican, not forgetting our seeming dogged refusal to have Confessions? Is there a residuum of ritual that can be called Anglican, bearing in mind the fact that every ritual bears the marks of a context, be it culture or otherwise? And if there is such a residuum of Anglican religious experience, belief and ritual, can it and must it be expressed in the same way everywhere in the Communion? And if there is room for different expressions, what then are the legitimate limits of differentiation and diversity within the one Communion? When does difference become division? In putting such questions it is not the intention to exclude one or the other. One is seeking to do two things at the same time:

The Plenary Presentations

on the one hand, to affirm immense, God-given diversity; on the other, to deny that for that reason anything goes. I will return to these questions in a little while.

For now I wish to turn to another aspect of describing the Anglican Communion as a religious phenomenon. Today we are more than conscious that the Anglican Communion stands in the context of religious pluralism. In parts of the Communion Anglicanism is one institutional face of Christianity alongside Islam, Buddhism, Hinduism, Baha'i, African Traditional Religions, etc. Our dioceses in the Gambia, Sierra Leone, Sudan, Malaysia, live as minorities in predominantly Muslim nations. Even Britain, which has had established Anglicanism, is now conscious of Muslims in Bradford, Sikhs in London, etc. The search for Anglican identity today then is done in a context also of inter-faith relationship which will foster the search for community of communities, in short, in a world community. Hans Gensichen, a German Lutheran theologian, has written:

> No analysis of the present situation and no approach to a new world community can afford to ignore the problems posed by the plurality of religions, nor should the dignity of religion and religions be disregarded by reducing them to means to an end and simply treating them as tools which may be used for a certain purpose and discarded. The elevation of inter-faith relationship to the rank of a world problem is and remains a necessity if mankind is at all to overcome its present divisions, religious and otherwise. What is needed above all else is, in the first place, a full measure of realism which is able to take into account both the existing religions as they are, in their particularity and peculiarity and the shock of secularism which is leading the religions to a reappraisal of their heritage which, again, will bear the peculiar stamp of the respective religion. This, after all, is what is primarily meant by the principle of tolerance; that people in other religions are taken seriously as adherents of that particular religion, without forcing them into decisions which they themselves are not prepared to take.[6]

I quote in extenso the words of Gensichen while I think of one of our dioceses in the Gambia, Nigeria, Sudan, Malaysia, India. Our search for the fundamentals of our Communion must not be just exclusivist; it must foster as well the community of communities in the one world which the one God has made (Psalm 24.1). But I do recall some words of Cardinal Newman: 'Oh how we hate one another for the love of God!' Where is the irenic potential of Christianity and, indeed, of other religions as we embark on the task of creating a world community? Gensichen adds:

> The time has long passed when Christianity could reasonably hope to win other people by decrying other religions outright or declaring them to be the inventions of the devil. Today, Christians will have to realise first of all that they, like people in other religions and secular ideologies, are all involved in the struggle

for the common humanity of the future, that they not only must co-exist with the other spiritual forces but that they have to co-operate with them in an endeavour to build the structure of a world community. In such genuine solidarity for the sake of their fellow men Christians should not allow themselves to be outdone by anyone. It is, after all, this very message of God the Creator and Sustainer of all men which should stimulate Christians to do everything in their power to participate in the cause of freedom, justice and human rights everywhere, and thus actively to contribute to the new movement of human solidarity'.[7]

We search for our Anglican identity (or even identities) not as an autonomous entity unaffected by the world around us, but in the context of religious pluralism in which each religion seeks to commend itself to humanity and each of which claims to be working for the wellbeing of humanity. Let not the search for Anglican identity be an exercise in exclusion but an exercise in and of inclusion. And I dare say that is what the Anglican via media in its own way signalled – a commitment to inclusiveness and inclusivity.

ANGLICAN COMMUNION AS A CHRISTIAN EXPERIENCE AND EXPRESSION

Let me move from situating Anglicanism in the broader context of religious pluralism, to the narrower context of Christian pluralism. Anglicanism makes no claim to be *the* church. Indeed, the self-description of Anglicanism as via media is a commitment to avoiding extremes and affirming peoples and institutions across the board, a commitment to talking round every issue, seeing inherent merits and demerits across the board. It is a commitment to provisionality and tolerance. This is our style and it binds us together in one Communion in spite of our regional, cultural and racial differences. I guess I am saying I am first an African, then a Christian and then an Anglican.

Europeans, especially Germans, often get uncomfortable with the language of 'I am first an African, and second a Christian'. The German disquiet is due to their unfortunate experience of persecution and compromise of the faith related to German Christianity under Hitler. But I am afraid abuse does not do away with true use. The simple truth is I took in my Africanness with my mother's milk, long before I became a conscious Christian. Besides, the story of the incarnation informs us that the flesh with all its inclination to sinfulness and weakness is, nevertheless, part of the stuff in which God encounters us. Let us not be afraid to use a renewed African culture for our particular 'Anglican' expression, etc.

Let me develop this a little more. Our membership in Africa has come from a religious background other than Christian. *Homo africanus homo religiosus radicaliter*: i.e., the African is through and through religious and African cultures have a religious-spiritual epistemology and ontology. To be is to be religious and 'mystical values' intrude into their systems of maintaining law and order. These Africans come to Anglicanism with some religious values inextricably mixed up with the cultures. To ignore that reality is to pretend to something that is not possible. This is why the issues of polygamy, ancestral rites, etc., are still on our agenda.

What are the peculiar Anglican elements in that Christian spectrum?

1. *Establishment?* The Church of England was the English state church. The Act of Uniformity of 1559 re-established it as such. But it hardly needs to be said that the Communion does not have establishment as of its essence, although the spirit of establishment tends to dog its heels everywhere. In Ghana/Gold Coast the spirit of this establishment is evident in the description of that church as *aban mu asor* i.e. the church in the castle or church of the government. Bishop John Daly, Bishop of Accra, 1950-54 writes: 'When I arrived in Accra I discovered that the Bishop was driven by a uniformed chauffeur in a fine Mercedes'.[8]

On this I have commented as follows: 'Needless to say, the church leadership had been accommodated to the colonial administration. To ride a Mercedes in a poor church was hardly a mark of the church of the poor'.[9] Be that as it may, in an age when we have rediscovered God's preferential option for the poor, the spirit of establishment needs to be critically assessed, if not exorcised. In any case in the new consciousness of the ecumenical imperative the establishment of one church or religion as official religion of the nation needs careful and sensitive re-examination.

2. *Articles of Religion?* In 1553 the 42 Articles of Religion were designed as a Confession of Faith. It was revised in 1563 as the 39 Articles. It used to be the case that people, even in Africa, made affirmation of these at their ordination. There is the debate as to whether they are to be accepted as a confession of faith or a general agreement in the sense of boundaries which are not to be transgressed. In any case, the 39 Articles are hardly in active use in our Communion; they stand as part of our tradition but not something we stand or fall by. But let me pose a question: as we define ourselves anew is it desirable to have a confession of faith as the general fence around what we stand by? Would we consider articles of religion as a statement of our basic Anglicanism? If not, how else do we clearly define ourselves?

Philip H. E. Thomas wrote a paper in 1985 on *The Status and Function of the Thirty-Nine Articles in the Anglican Communion Today*. He concluded as follows: 'Plainly the Thirty-Nine Articles are not the focus of attention for many Anglicans. Their actual status and function varies from place to place, between one ecclesiastical pressure group or another, and among different individuals in the Anglican Communion. For the great majority of Anglican Christians they will not seem particularly accessible or important. Nevertheless the Articles cannot be entirely lost from present-day consciousness. No responsible account of the Anglican tradition can ignore their existence. They are not intended to provide answers "from the back of the book", but they do still hold an honourable and significant place in the varied textures of Anglican theological debate. Anglicanism cannot be defined by reference to the Articles alone, but it cannot be understood fully without them.' Let me add my personal comment that this is a sober judgement which obliges us to reassess what the 39 Articles really represent today, especially as we face others who have defined their identity in Confessions.

3. *Book of Common Prayer?* This is a significant event of the English Reformation, published in 1549 and revised in 1552. As it happens, it is the one enduring item of the Anglican Communion. Even the Book of Common Prayer of the Episcopal Church of the USA, after all the alterations necessary in their context, does not 'depart from the Church of England in any essential point of doctrine, discipline or worship' (from the Preface). But what does it mean to acknowledge it as the one enduring thing of Anglicanism?

4. *Episcopacy as 'the source and centre of our order'?* That is not the problem, because I believe it is part of the catholic tradition. The issue is the model of episcopacy which in our history has often been modelled on the English aristocracy – a model that is not in place in every part of the Communion.

Anglicans are committed to dispersed authority.[10] This set us apart from the Roman Catholics. We are sold on the tradition from fairly early times (about the fourth century in Africa) that the bishop is supreme in his diocese and possesses ordinary jurisdiction with regard to teaching, governing, adjudicating, and administration of sacraments. But what is the cash value of such affirmations?

ANGLICAN COMMUNION AS A FEATURE OF ECUMENICAL MOVEMENT

We describe ourselves as a Communion. But the ecumenical movement has rediscovered the basic ecclesiology to be Koinonia, a Greek word which means both community and communion.[11] The word was given ecu-

His Grace the Archbishop of Canterbury with His Holiness Pope John Paul II at the Vatican in 1992

Towards a Renewed Vision

menical visibility by a 1920 call from the Ecumenical Patriarchate for the establishment of 'koinonia of churches' a fellowship or communion of churches, in spite of the doctrinal differences between the churches. On this call, W. A. Visser 't Hooft, the first General Secretary of the World Council of Churches, commented: 'The Church of Constantinople was among the first to remind us that the world of Christendom would be disobedient to the will of the Lord and Saviour if it did not seek to manifest in the world the unity of the people of God and of the body of Christ'.[12] The self-definition of the Anglican Communion is to attempt to define which limb it is in the community/communion of churches, alongside Roman Catholics, Methodists, Reformed, Lutheran, Greek and Oriental Orthodox, etc. In the nature of koinonia, such definition should not be reactionary but complementary to other definitions. What is Anglican Communion *vis à vis* the Communion of churches?

Traditionally Anglicans answered the foregoing question in terms of the via media. John Howe, who in this forum needs no introduction, has written: 'One can contend that the role that was often accorded to Anglicanism by Anglicans is largely on the basis of being episcopal and reformed – that is a "bridge" church – carries less conviction than it did. There is a wider disposition that the high road to reunion is seldom established by building bridges: progress by convergence has become a more acceptable highway.'[13]

However, as Henry Chadwick has commented, the via media signals something deeper: 'In dialogue with Protestants the Anglicans must resist the temptation to reduce the strong Catholic elements in Anglicanism. Likewise, in dialogue with Orthodox or Roman Catholic theologians the evangelical elements (justification by faith and the primacy of Scripture) which were and still are essential for Anglican thought cannot be disparaged'.[14]

This brings us to the other Anglican fond note, Catholic and Protestant. As a Protestant body we take the Bible seriously. Article VI of the 39 Articles, *Of the Sufficiency of the Holy Scriptures for Salvation* puts us firmly in the Protestant tradition. It reads, 'Holy Scripture containeth all things necessary to salvation: so that whatsoever is not read therein, nor may be proved thereby, is not required of any man, that it should be believed as an article of Faith, or be thought requisite or necessary to salvation.' Let me hasten to add that if serious engagement with Scripture is a trait of Protestantism, it is also a mark of the Catholic tradition. For Scripture belongs to the common wealth of Christians of whatever description. However, beyond the basic agreement and affirmation, we need to struggle on how to read scripture. Churches of the South are arguing for new eyes for reading, reading scripture from the perspective of God's preferential option for the poor. This style does not sit well with many from the North. But I only mention it here to signal that there is a real difference between North and South on the style of doing theology which is not peculiar to us Anglicans.

Rejection of centralised authority is also another link with the Protestant tradition. That has been mentioned above. This has regained added importance because of the rediscovery of the church as the people of God. But that is inextricably linked with a Catholic tradition of commitment to episcopacy.

From as early as Ignatius of Antioch (*c*.AD 107-10), there was steady exhortation to obedience in the church and respect for the bishop. In the words of Rowan Williams, 'the bishop is the figure who guarantees the harmony of the church by gathering it around him to celebrate the eucharist, and this eucharistic harmony is the assurance and expression of a true harmony with the will of God, or the "mind" of God as embodied in Jesus (Ephesians III-V, Smyrnaeans VIII, Philadelphians I)'.[15] At least this is the theory. We need to make the theory the experience of parishioners, if it is not already their experience.

However, Anglicans balance episcopacy with the participation of the people of God, at least in theory. And so, there is synodical government which 'was designed to achieve a more effective and coherent system, to give a greater part to the laity . . .'.[16] The interesting thing to note is that for the Church of England it came in only with the Synodical Government Measure of 1969. Before then Australia was practising it. Indeed, already in 1893 there was a General Synod in Canada. To that extent Britain was a latecomer to synodical government and has learned from other parts of the Communion. And now the Roman church also is learning even if seemingly grudgingly, to give cash value to its rediscovery of the church as the people of God. The actual models of this commitment to episcopacy and the commitment to people's participation is something we need to struggle with at the diocesan, provincial and Communion-wide levels. That is why we are struggling with the role of Primates' meeting, and Lambeth.

This is where I wish to mention the role of the Bishop of the See of Canterbury in the Communion. That he will become the Anglican pope is not on. Traditionally we have described him as *Primus inter pares*, the first among equals. There is debate about whether this primus must always be Canterbury. Some respond positively because Canterbury is 'the spiritual home' of Anglicans, a language that does not sit well with several Anglicans. Where am I in all this?

According to sociologists, a community has a focus of identification, like a chief. So the primus is a symbol of the unity, solidarity, permanence, continuity and perfection. In this regard and in some countries 'mystical values' or symbolic values intrude in the system of maintaining law and order. Coming as I do from an African background, I see the primus as, to use the language of the sociologists, 'double pivot', i.e., the political head of the tribe and the centre of its ritual expression.[17] This sacral quality derives from the sociological fact that the primus symbolises the whole society and is for that reason raised to a mystical plane. Let us not 'poohpooh' this mystical element as an undergirding factor of structures. If only you will pause for a moment to reflect, you will probably agree that we humans are incurable for our penchant for the mystical. I suggest that such mystique already attaches itself to the beginnings at Canterbury which becomes the symbol of our permanence and solidarity. The See of St Augustine can then become the symbol of unity, solidarity, permanence, continuity, and our striving for perfection. In any event a communion like the Anglican Communion is better served by a focus of identification, like a primus inter pares.

What do I personally make of the matter of Catholicity? The Anglican Communion belongs to the una sancta, the one holy, catholic and apostolic church, whose basic ecclesiology has been rediscovered as koinonia. Thus there is a fundamental Christian bond between us and all other Christians. It is the elements of this common bond that we describe as Catholicity. We do not define Catholicity by the Roman Catholic Church. The common wealth includes the common belief in the Trinity, common commitment and nourishment by Scripture, common consecration by baptism in the threefold name, common special regard for eucharist, in our adherence to the sacraments of baptism and eucharist. We need to seek our identity through the renewed ecumenical convergence on baptism and eucharist. The sacraments bind us to other Christians. Baptism, Eucharist, Ministry (BEM) brings us to a renewed theology of baptism which carries with it a renewed theology of ministry, especially the priesthood of all believers. So far as I am concerned, the priesthood of all believers has significance only if it is inextricably linked with the mission of the people of God. Sacramental theology is not limited to the temple but is also the liturgy after the liturgy. Sacramental life is not just ritual or dogma or just a meal. It involves and is bound up with a dynamic, historical dimension. It is concerned with real change in social, economic and political life – Rom. 6.3f; Luke 4.18-19.

Koinonia is not mere companionship between people. Neither is it just good fellowship of a society or club. Nor is it just community, i.e., society. Rather it is *participation*, having a joint share. 'The Church is essentially a community, a fellowship. But it is by participating together in the Holy Spirit of God and in the character he imparts that Christians come to be thus bound together into a fellowship. And 'sharing' together in the Holy Spirit carries in it the promise of God's future crowning of his purpose. It is thus that one day his purpose will be completed and his kingship established through the Church.'[18] Does each diocese, province and individual Anglican feel a share in what the Communion is about? Or are some spectators, if not addenda, to a show going on elsewhere?

The identity of the Anglican Communion is then in part to be sought in the ecumenical movement which is the institutional form of the understanding of the Church as koinonia. It will be verified when the Anglicans participate with others in being the one body of Christ which is together in mission and together are obedient to the will of God so as to bring the totality of life and creation under God's sovereign rule.

Let me now attempt to draw threads together. We search for a renewed identity for new times, not only for our own sake but also for the sake of our faithfulness in mission to the world. The mission is to a world in the grip of science and technology, which in spite of its very positive contributions implies values and an anthropology which at the very least are inconsistent with our faith in parts. It is to a world in which there is much poverty, deprivation, marginalisation and suffering. It is to a world of tremendous pluralism of religions, cultures, gender, sexual tastes. It is to a world in which in spite of everything there is tremendous spiritual yearning. We do so at a time when we are confronted by crises of faith, crises of church and crises of world, which call for the cutting edges of mission in today's world to be more clearly identified and defined. It is this missionary vision that should in part, at any rate, determine the instrument that is required to do the job.

Some Three Questions

We need to face three questions as a communion: what does it look like to be church in a communion? What does it look like to be a communion in mission in today's world? What does it look like for the communion to be obedient to the will of God in the social, economic and political realities, recognising that these are some of the contours of the ethical imperative of God's rule? There is an interesting example of the oneness in obedience to the will of God which I cannot resist recalling here. Archbishop Robert Runcie spoke at a Press Conference in Montreal, Canada which was reported in the *Church Times*, 13 September 1985 (p. 1). He was addressing the solidarity of the Communion with the church in South Africa in the bleak days of apartheid. He said: 'If you touch Desmond Tutu you do not just touch somebody in South Africa, but a world family is involved.' This expression can be repeated in Myanmar, in the Sudan, etc. When we answer those questions the theologians may reflect and deduce a theology of being communion in a wider communion. This brings me to my last point: the nature of theology.

Nature of Theologising in the Communion

Our theological roots are in the North. There theology has been done in a propositional form. Churches of the South are saying that is not the only style, and indeed, is rather deadly. Theology can be couched as story, art, dance, music. The Communion must learn to state its belief in these other ways as well.

Second, traditional theology has always assumed that reality may be perceived everywhere in the same way. And so you always started from some constants like God, church, sin, etc. In a global village in which we are obliged to learn from others, from other cultures, we are having to review the basic tenets of our faith. But more importantly, we are learning that reality is best gleaned from social relationships and not just from ideas. The Communion must begin to describe its theology on the basis of the existing relationships between congregations, dioceses.

Third, theology is not just a scientific discipline; it serves the mission of the church and must, therefore, be informed by the missionary perspective.

Finally, the theology of an established church, and indeed from before, had been informed by the Christendom ideology. With the rediscovery of God's preferential option for the poor, that becomes the perspective and test of our being church. What does God's preferential option for the poor mean for our identity as Anglican Communion on one mission?

ENDNOTES

1 W. O. B. Allen-E. McClure, *Two Hundred Years. The History of the Society for Promoting Christian Knowledge 1698-1898*, 1898; W.K. Lowther Clarke, *A History of SPCK*, 1959; C. F. Pascoe, *Two Hundred Years of the SPG (1701-1900)*, 1901; H. P. Thompson, *Into All Lands: History of the Society for the Propagation of the Gospel in Foreign Lands 1701-1950*, 1951; Margaret Dewey, *The Messengers*, London: A. R. Mowbray, 1975

2 W. S. Perry, ed. *Historical Collections Relating to the American Colonial Church 1870-78*; W. S. Perry, *The History of the American Episcopal Church 1587-1883*, 2 volumes, Boston 1885. C. C. Tiffany, *A History of the Protestant Episcopal Church in the USA*, New York, 1895.

The Plenary Presentations

3. Eugene Stock, *The History of the Church Missionary Society*, 3 volumes, 1899; G. Hewitt, *The Problems of Success. A History of the Church Missionary Society 1900-1942*, 2 volumes, 1971-7.
4. Orlando Costas, *The Integrity of Mission*, London: Harper and Row, 1979
5. I. M. Lewis, *Ecstatic Religion, An Anthropological Study of Spirit Possession and Shamanism*, Harmondsworth, 1971
6. H.W. Gensichen, 'World Community and World Religions' in *Religion in a Pluralistic Society*, ed. J. S. Pobee, Leiden: E. J. Brill, 1976, pp. 34-5
7. *ibid.*, p. 36
8. John C. S. Daly, *Four Mitres. Reminiscences of an Irresponsible Bishop*, part III, n.d., p.9
9. John S. Pobee, *A.D. 2000 and After: the Future of God's Mission in Africa*, Accra: Asempa Press, 1991, p.42
10. Stephen W. Sykes, *The Integrity of Anglicanism* London: Mowbury, 1979, p. 89
11. F. Hauck, 'Koinonia', *Dictionary of the New Testament*, Grand Rapids: Wm. Eerdmans, 1989: pp. 789-809; André Birmelé et. al., *Communio-Koinonia*, Strasbourg: Institute for Ecumenical Studies, 1990; ARCIC II, *Church as Communion*.
12. W. A. Visser 't Hooft, 'Celui qui n'assemble pas avec moi disperse', Sermon at St Peter's Cathedral, Geneva, 8 November 1967, on the occasion of the visit of the Ecumenical Patriarch Athenagoras. See also Visser 't Hooft, *The Genesis and Formation of the World Council of Churches*, Geneva: WCC, 1982, pp.1-8
13. John Howe, *Highways and Hedges : Anglicanism and the Universal Church* London: CIO, 1985, pp.114
14. Cited in K. Aland, *A History of Christianity from the Reformation to the Present*, Vol. 2, Philadelphia: Fortress Press, 1986, p.362
15. Rowan Williams, 'Ignatius of Antioch, St', *A Dictionary of Christian Spirituality*, ed. G. S. Wakefield, London: SCM, 1983, pp.205-66
16. F. L. Cross (ed.), *The Oxford Dictionary of the Christian Church*, revised, Oxford: OUP, 1990, p.1332
17. See E. E. Evans-Pritchard, 'The Divine Kingship of the Shilluk of the Nilotic Sudan: the Frazer Lecture, 1948', *Social Anthropology and Other Essays*, New York: The Free Press of Glencoe, 1962, p.210
18. C. F. D. Moule, *Christ's Messengers*, New York: Association Press, 1957, p.73; J. Y. Campbell, 'Koinonia and its Cognates in the New Testament'. *Three New Testament Studies*, Leiden: E. J. Brill, 1965, pp.3-28

The Sermons
by
The Archbishop of Canterbury

The Good Hope Centre, Cape Town
Day of Celebration Eucharist
24 January 1993

Jesus was walking by the Sea of Galilee when he saw two brothers, Simon called Peter and his brother Andrew, casting a net into the lake; for they were fishermen. Jesus said to them, 'Come with me, and I will make you fishers of men.' (Matthew 4)

Today is a great day for our Anglican Communion. At last a gathering of representatives from every Anglican Church around the world is able to meet in this wonderful land. We are thrilled to be with you in South Africa and in this glorious city of Cape Town.

It is in fact an historic moment for us to greet you together, our dear sisters and brothers in the Church of the Province of Southern Africa, and to do so without hindrance or anxiety. We rejoice with you and the whole Christian community in South Africa, and we salute our gracious and generous host today, your beloved Archbishop Desmond.

We have called today a Day of Celebration in our Conference programme. Conferences and committees are hard work, and yet Anglicans seem particularly prone to them. They strain our patience and it is good to take a break, to stand back, and celebrate the faith that we share together. This is my first visit to South Africa – indeed to any part of Africa – so it is a special pleasure to be with you. I have already discovered that when it comes to celebration, there is a lot you can teach me, and you will find me an enthusiastic pupil. Every Sunday is a Day of Celebration, a celebration of the victory of Jesus Christ over the forces of darkness.

And we meet today in the Good Hope Centre, a name that has been familiar to me since childhood. I realise it's a name that may sound a note of irony in the hearts of many South Africans, but there could be no better name for a place of Christian celebration. Every Sunday is a celebration of victory: every Eucharist is a centre of good hope – reliable hope, unquenchable hope in the name of Jesus Christ. Because it is Jesus who calls us out of darkness into his own marvellous light.

So we meet as resurrection people to celebrate the triumph of hope and the fulfilment of God's promise. Whether we live in the Cape of Good Hope, on the shores of Lake Galilee or Lake Malawi, or by the waters of the Nile, the Zambezi or the South China Sea, Jesus calls us to a life of cel-

The Cape Eucharist

ebration and service. He says, 'Come with me and I will make you fishers of men.'

Let's look for the moment at what is implied by those famous words. First, the call of Jesus is personal and simple. He spoke directly, simply and personally to two people. The Gospel writer Matthew does not tell us much about how it happened. We know little in detail about the way Jesus addressed the first disciples. Was it imperious command or gentle invitation? Did Jesus plead with them or persuade them to follow him? What was it about him that made Simon and Andrew drop their nets at once and follow him? And what did he mean by that phrase 'fishers of men'? But they did not stop to answer such tantalising questions; without hesitation they abandoned their livelihood for an unknown future. We are left to conclude that it was the commanding authority of Jesus that ruled out any questions, any doubts or delay. 'Come,' he said, 'Come with me.'

There is a simplicity about our Christian vocation. We come to you today from all corners of the globe. Anglicans are to be found in every continent, in every culture and climate, and it has been my privilege to meet you during these past two years in the refugee camps of Sri Lanka, in the homes of beleaguered Palestinians on the West Bank, in mountain villages of Papua New Guinea, as well as among the towers of Manhattan, London, and Hong Kong. We are proud of our cultural diversity, and we welcome the variety of our membership. We know that the Gospel requires of us different tasks in different places.

But perhaps we don't sufficiently acknowledge that what unites us is so simple. It is this: Christ has called each of us by name to follow his way. Each of us has been called individually: Elizabeth, Simon, Mary, Andrew. We are a band of people 'whose hearts God has touched'. He has laid his hand upon us. All of us can look back to a time – perhaps many times – when Christ beckoned us, and we took our first faltering steps along his way. He called us – urgently, insistently, or repeatedly – and we followed, enthusiastically, gladly, immediately. Our first duty as followers of Jesus is to remain faithful to that call, to cherish and celebrate our vocation, to stay close to Jesus Christ, by prayer and holiness of life.

Second, Christ called his followers together. We are a fellowship of Christians and a fellowship of Churches. We belong to one another. We rejoice with those who rejoice and we weep with those who weep. We talk a lot about Communion these days, and we try to overcome our doctrinal disagreements. But our Communion is just as much impaired by our failure to bear one another's burdens – whether it is the burden of political oppression, economic deprivation, or secular apathy. When Jesus called us, he called us together, and to care for one another.

Few people can be unmoved today by the terrible suffering that afflicts

The Sermons

the great continent of Africa. Africa lies wounded and bleeding, and we who live elsewhere must not pass by on the other side. No Christian can be excused from coming to the aid of our African brothers and sisters in need.

The world needs a new vision of Africa. We need a new spirit of repentance, a new sense of responsibility, a new determination to express our common humanity by just and fair dealing between our nations. We cannot claim to obey Christ's call and follow him if we neglect those who walk with us.

We meet on the African continent where 16 of the poorest countries of the world are to be found. We Anglicans are in these countries. We know their anguish at first hand.

Today we meet in a country where the scourge of apartheid has left deep scars of violence, shame and anger on black and white alike. Anglicans are united in resenting the injustice and economic deprivation that Africans have inherited. We stand for dignity, equality and justice, for that is the will of the one who calls us to walk with him.

Yet Africa deserves our gratitude, as well as our help. We rejoice in the wonderful humanity and generosity of spirit that Africa offers the world through its peoples. We thank God for your Christ-like capacity for forgiveness. By his grace you are putting the past behind you in South Africa. You are discovering Christ in one another. You are allowing Christ to reach you across the old racial divide. You are able to receive each other's gifts and graces. You are creating a single new humanity out of the blasphemies of the past. I want you to know that your Anglican friends are with you – because together we have followed the call of Jesus Christ to walk with him.

Third, Jesus said, 'Come *with me*'. The call of Jesus is a call to walk with him, to accompany him, to be by his side. I like the idea of a shared pilgrimage; it suggests a destiny ahead, an adventure, an exploration. Jesus does not stand still; he is with us on our journey, leading us as our guide and our companion. He will choose the route, and we are not to mind whether it is steep or flat, narrow or wide, rough or smooth. Few churches have walked so stony and testing a path as the Church of the Province in recent years, but you have not halted or strayed or turned back. You have wrestled with the issues and dilemmas of conscience, you have suffered persecution and hardship and the whole Christian world has been blessed by your witness. Jesus said, 'Come with me', and you stayed by him.

Faithful discipleship discovers that there is no hardship which cannot be endured by those whose hearts are fixed on him. We know there are no easy solutions or slick answers for Christians who follow Jesus into the turbulence and tumults of public life; we also know that it is there above all places that the message of Christ's kingdom and peace must be proclaimed. 'Come with me,' says Christ, 'and I will never leave you.'

Finally, Jesus said, 'I will make you fishers of men.' He calls us by name, he calls us together, he calls us to be with him, and he gives us a commission to become fishers of men.

Many people in my own country are shy of becoming fishermen or women, at least in their own society. They mistakenly believe that you can be a Christian without being a missionary. This is not so. A faith not shared is a faith not understood. We are faced today, perhaps as never before, with the need for Christians to be confident in what they believe, keen to bring others to Christ, and ready to commit themselves in wholehearted discipleship. I sense around our Communion today a refreshing shaking-off of Anglican – or should I say English – reserve. In this Decade of Evangelism we are learning not to be ashamed to confess the faith of Christ crucified. We are finding that when we walk with Christ, he turns us into new people. He takes our gifts and moulds them in his service. His Spirit works on us, shaping us, equipping us for ministry and mission.

So we come, his children called to be with him, to this holy table. As we offer bread and wine, so we offer ourselves in joyful obedience to his service, asking him to take us as we are, to bless us, and to make us into what he wants.

You see, it is all about commitment. One man who inspired millions of people was Martin Luther King Jr. After his death his wife Coretta wrote these words: 'My husband often told the children that if a man had nothing that was worth dying for, then he was not fit to live. He also said that what really matters is not *how* you live, but how *well* you live.'

May the same Lord that inspired Martin Luther King Jr give us the grace to live well for him and his kingdom, to follow him gladly and joyfully, and to give ourselves to his service.

St George's Cathedral, Cape Town
Solemn Sung Mass
Sunday 31 January 1993

I begin by saying how delighted I am to be with you this morning. It seems so natural that my final service here in South Africa should be in the Cathedral Church of St George's, Cape Town, with your Archbishop Desmond Tutu celebrating. And how splendid to accompany the Holy Eucharist with Mozart's glorious *Coronation Mass*. It is one that is often sung in Canterbury Cathedral and I must say that the performance we have heard and enjoyed this morning, and which has so richly added to our worship, matches any I have heard before.

But there is another reason why I am glad to be here. This Cathedral has been in the forefront of resistance to apartheid. You are part of the irresistible advance towards the goal of non-racial democracy. The clergy and people of this place have stood alongside all those who are determined to bring social and structural change by peaceful means. On Wednesday I visited people in Khayalitsha, and I was told there how some of them were

St George's Cathedral

known as 'Cathedral Squatters'. I learned how a few years ago women whose husbands were in hostels appealed to the Cathedral for refuge, how a vigil was held here, and a haven provided. That told me something of your ministry, as a place of hope and practical help. Of course much remains to be done and I believe that the Gospel we heard just a moment ago offers some insights that we do well to heed.

The story is familiar to us. The disciples are in a boat and crossing the usually peaceful Lake Galilee. A storm erupts and the boat is quickly swamped. The terrified disciples, thinking their last moments have arrived, appeal to the Lord for help. He calms them and the storm abates. They are stunned by his authority: 'What kind of man is this, that even the winds and the sea obey him?'

The passage deals with three fundamental qualities of Christian discipleship, which I would like to consider with you this morning – three capacities which all Christians need to develop: the capacity to overcome fear, the capacity to believe, and the capacity to follow.

First, consider the *fear*. They had good reason to be afraid and we may well believe we have too. There are many differences between my society and yours but there are many similarities too. Please don't allow visitors to get away with the idea that their societies are perfect and yours is not. One of the odious consequences of apartheid has been the self-righteousness that it has made some non-South Africans feel about their own countries. In fact we share many of the same problems – unemployment, racial prejudice and violence. No society – and no Church – is perfect. And when we are confronted with problems we immediately dread the worst. We see the storm clouds, we feel the gusts of wind, and we are terrified. All are agreed that here the problems are daunting in their size and complexity. There is vast unemployment, terrible housing conditions, and devastating violence. Apartheid has been discredited as an inhuman and intolerable political system, unworthy of any civilised society, but a full electoral democracy has yet to replace it. Much remains to be done, and many dangers lie ahead. It is only natural that we should tremble. Like the disciples on Lake Galilee, squalls may hit us, and threaten to capsize the ship, and drown our hopes.

Central to fear is the fear of the unknown. What will it be like to have a shift of power? We may all wish to see change – but it is folly to think that a new dispensation will bring sudden health and happiness to all. In such circumstances apprehension and fear are natural and understandable.

But the Christian is used to change. It was J. F. Kennedy who once remarked: 'The only certain and immutable thing is that nothing in this life is certain and immutable.' We Christians do not put our faith in political systems, we are pilgrims seeking a city which is to come. At the centre of

The Sermons

our faith is the rock-like certainty that Jesus Christ is the same, yesterday, today and forever. Our security, our resources, our strength, do not ultimately depend on politicians; our hope lies in the life of the Kingdom of God, and in the fellowship of his Son.

Churches have to face up to change, too. The Western world is no longer uniformly Christian; we are surrounded by adherents of other faiths whose sincerity and devotion is not a whit inferior to ours. We must learn new forms of sharing our faith; co-operating wherever we can and learning to tolerate in love. It is not easy – but then again change is never easy.

So the capacity to overcome fear is directly related to our willingness to look in the right direction – to look to our Lord. The disciples looked at the storms and trembled. When they started to look to him things began to happen. He was in control.

In the last century, off the coast of South West England (Cornwall), a liner went down and many people were drowned. The paper reported the remarkable story of a galley boy of 16 who somehow was thrown on the rocks and managed to survive until morning. He was asked by a foolish reporter: 'Didn't you tremble all night as you clung for safety?' He replied: 'Yes, of course I did. But do you know – the rock never trembled once!'

Then I notice the *capacity to believe*. 'Lord, save us, we are perishing,' and he replied: 'Why are you afraid, you of little faith?'. Perhaps it is natural too for us to doubt at moments of deep darkness. Some here have been through the valley of the shadow of death – bereavement, deep anxiety or personal loss – and you will know the harrowing experience of having nothing to cling to. It is a fact however that the storm often provides the opportunity to rediscover faith; the moment for a dormant faith to flower into a tough reliance on God and his presence with us through the storms. But faith is far more than wishful thinking or a pious hope that somehow God might get us out of trouble. Faith is to do with the direction of our gaze; it is not a last resort to which we turn when all else fails. Faith is the capacity of our minds to trust in a Creator who has created this amazing universe. Faith is the capacity to reach out to him to share in his work of recreation. Faith is the capacity to see the world as he sees it, to identify with his concerns, his moral judgements and requirements. As St Teresa said so splendidly long ago: 'The best way of knowing God is to frequent the company of his friends.'

The capacity to believe in God must therefore entertain the possibility that he can create a new social order among you, an order which begins with the conviction that *all* are made in the image and likeness of God; I believe God has given you a special opportunity here to witness to his power of forgiveness, of renewal and redemption. Let God design the new South Africa, for your children and your children's children. Let him be the architect of a future South Africa that will be just and fair to all.

St George's Cathedral

Last of all I notice in the passage a challenge for us to have the *capacity to follow*. (It is in fact the whole point of the mysterious extract just before the storm on the lake in which Jesus said: 'Let the dead bury the dead – follow me!') The episode of the storm underlines the nature of our vocation. We are challenged to follow the Man of Galilee who calls us through the storms of life to mature faith and to costly service. That is what this Cathedral and the Church in this land stand for. We are not here because we are simply interested in music or church architecture – wonderful though they may be. Our devotion derives from a deeper centre; that of following our Lord through thick and thin. No one is beyond the reach of God's love. No situation is beyond his power to redeem. So we never despair when the clouds are grey, or the sea is rough. That is precisely when the Church and the Christian can find again their inspiring centre of hope and courage. In the Gospel the disciples marvelled when their Lord stilled the storm. 'What sort of man is this!' they said. That is a cry which still breaks from the lips of his followers. Our God is a God of surprises. Like a magnet he draws us to him – to discover the source of his power, to be changed by his love, and then to take sides with him. Christ changes societies and communities, and transforms hearts and lives. He calls – and we gladly follow him.

The theme of the Primates Meeting and the Anglican Consultative Council these past two weeks has been 'A Transforming Vision'. The vision is Christ. It is he who can transform the world, and make us unafraid in his presence.

Tomorrow I shall leave the Cape of Good Hope – once known as the Cape of Storms – and return to England. I shall go with a full and overflowing heart. I shall go with my vision renewed by all that Christian people are doing here. I am grateful to God for all his gifts to you, and above all for your abundant faith and hope in the transforming power of Jesus Christ. To him be the glory.

Resolutions

RESOLUTIONS OF THE JOINT MEETING OF THE PRIMATES OF THE ANGLICAN COMMUNION AND THE ANGLICAN CONSULTATIVE COUNCIL JANUARY 1993

Resolution 1 - Christian Unity

Resolved, that this Joint Meeting of the Primates of the Anglican Communion and the Anglican Consultative Council affirms the unity in Christ of all Christians, and our commitment to work for the reconciliation of the churches.

Resolution 2 - World Council of Churches

Resolved, that this Joint Meeting of the Primates of the Anglican Communion and the Anglican Consultative Council affirms its support of the World Council of Churches and recommends that the Provinces of the Anglican Communion respond seriously to the study book on the Understanding and Vision of the World Council of Churches to be distributed in 1993, and that copies of these responses be sent to the Anglican Communion Office;

That an *ad hoc* group be gathered for a study of the relationship between the World Council of Churches and the Anglican Communion, along with other Communions within the total ecumenical movement; and the report of this group be sent to the Provinces for further comment before a final document is presented to the Anglican Communion and the WCC through the ACC.

Resolution 3 - Relations with the Roman Catholic Church

Resolved, that this Joint Meeting of the Primates of the Anglican Communion and the Anglican Consultative Council, while acknowledging that there has been widespread Anglican disappointment with the official Roman Catholic response to the ARCIC I Final Report, issued on 5 December 1991, nevertheless gives thanks to God that, throughout the Anglican Communion, local initiatives with Roman Catholics are being maintained and in some Provinces are increasing; takes note of new initiatives particularly in inter-church families, clergy conferences, joint theological education, co-operation of bishops, movement of clergy (noting the Canadian pastoral guidelines), common witness, and service in the local community.

Encourages the development of local initiatives on a wide range of issues and urges those engaged in them to reflect on their theological significance, the sharing of this work between the churches of the Anglican Communion and the Anglican members of ARCIC II to be facilitated by the Ecumenical Secretary.

Recommends that ARCIC II proceed as a matter of priority with its mandate to give attention to the official responses of both Churches, as well as the issue of methodology raised by the Archbishop of Canterbury.

Resolution 4 - Relations with the Oriental Orthodox

Resolved, that this Joint Meeting of the Primates of the Anglican Communion and the Anglican Consultative Council recommends that the next meeting of the Anglican/Oriental Orthodox Forum, meeting in May 1993, formulate in a clear and succinct statement, the agreement on Christology between Anglicans and the Oriental Orthodox Churches that was envisaged in the Communique of their last meeting. We proposed that the agreement may be brought by the Archbishop of Canterbury to the attention of the Member Churches of the Communion.

Resolution 5 - Relations with Baptists

Resolved, that this Joint Meeting of the Primates of the Anglican Communion and the Anglican Consultative Council notes the action taken by the Joint Standing Committees at Kanuga, 1992:

'that this Meeting resolves

(a) The underlying concern of Resolution 10 of the Lambeth Conference 1988 for growth in communion between Anglicans and Baptists be responded to:

   (i) by encouraging local dialogues and relationships between Baptists and Anglicans, recognising that an eventual international dialogue will need to be grounded in local experience;

   (ii) by learning from the reports and experience of the Baptist-Lutheran, Baptist-Reformed, Baptist-Mennonite, and Baptist-Roman Catholic dialogues, and that the possibility of sending an Anglican observer to a meeting of one or more of them be explored;

   (iii) by directing the ACC Ecumenical Secretary, or his nominee, to monitor these dialogues and the relationship with the Baptist World Alliance.

(b) The international dialogue between the Anglican Communion and the Baptist World Alliance be postponed, bearing in mind these proposals and the financial restraints facing the Inter-Anglican budget.'

Resolution 6 - Relations with the Orthodox

Resolved, that this Joint Meeting of the Primates of the Anglican Communion and the Anglican Consultative Council notes the action taken by the Joint Standing Committees at Kanuga, 1992:

'That this meeting resolves

(a) (i) as a matter of urgency and in the light of the long-standing and traditionally cordial relationships between the Anglican and Orthodox Churches, the Member Churches find ways of assisting the Orthodox Churches of Europe and the Commonwealth of Independent States. Such assistance could include material aid, provision of theological resources, scholarships and exchanges at various levels according to the request of the Churches themselves. Information should be shared with the Communion through the information services of the Anglican Communion Office;

   (ii) individual Member Churches consider the possibility of enter-

Resolutions of the Joint Meeting

           ing into partnership with specific Orthodox Churches, sharing the information through the Anglican Communion Office;
     (iii) in the light of the Orthodox Churches' misgivings about proselytism we offer the Orthodox Churches as much support as we can possibly offer to aid them in their work;
     (iv) the positive remarks about Anglican/Orthodox relations in the enthronement speech of the newly elected Ecumenical Patriarch be brought to the attention of the Member Churches.

(b) The Meeting welcomes the proposed series of annual Informal Talks to be inaugurated in June 1992 as a vehicle for overseeing the whole range of Anglican/Orthodox relations.

(c) The Meeting looks forward to receiving the results of the International Commission of Anglican-Orthodox Theological Dialogue's current discussions on ecclesiology and hopes that in its work the Commission will take note of other ecumenical agreements in this area.

(d) The Meeting welcomes the increasing implementation among the Member Churches of the Anglican Communion of the 1988 Lambeth Conference Resolution 6.5 (endorsed by Resolution 17 of ACC-8 in 1990) that "in future liturgical revisions the Niceno-Constantinopolitan Creed be printed without the Filioque clause".'

Resolution 7 - Relations with the Old Catholic Churches

Resolved, that this Joint Meeting of the Primates of the Anglican Communion and the Anglican Consultative Council recommends that

1. The ACC establish, together with the Old Catholic Churches of the Union of Utrecht, an Anglican/Old Catholic International Co-ordinating Council with the following purpose:

    (a) to study theological questions of continuing and mutual concern;
    (b) to address questions of co-operation and growth in mission and pastoral care, particularly in Europe;
    (c) to offer a model of continuing consultation and mutual support in pastoral care between Churches in communion, to other Churches approaching that stage in their life together.

2. The total membership be no more than 15 people to allow representatives from all the Churches of the Union and Anglican membership primarily from Europe and North America, with one or two Anglican members from other parts of the Anglican Communion.
3. The Commission have power to co-opt consultants as needed on a meeting-to-meeting basis.
4. The Inter-Anglican Budget set aside £5,000 in 1993 and £5,000 in 1996 towards the cost of the meeting, with a financial review no later than 1995.
5. The Council share reports of its meetings with the Anglican Communion through the Anglican Communion Office.

Resolution 8 - Relations with the Lutheran Churches

Resolved, that this Joint Meeting of the Primates of the Anglican Communion and the Anglican Consultative Council warmly welcomes the proposed Anglican/Lutheran Agreements in both the USA and Europe and recommends that the ACC:

Send to the Member Churches of the Anglican Communion and the Churches in Full Communion the text of the Episcopal-Lutheran dialogue in the USA, *Toward Full Communion and Concordat of Agreement, 1991* and *The Porvoo Common Statement*, the text of the conversations between the Church of England, the Church in Wales, the Episcopal Church of Scotland, the Church of Ireland and the Nordic and Baltic Lutheran Churches, together with the Apostolicity and Succession document of the Church of England by the end of 1993 for study, comment and report back to the Anglican Consultative Council and to the Provinces concerned.

Resolution 9 - Forum on Bilateral Dialogues

Resolved, that this Joint Meeting of the Primates of the Anglican Communion and the Anglican Consultative Council recommends the Christian World Communions convene the Forum on Bilateral Dialogues to study the methodology of ecumenism and the difficulties encountered in:

(a) the uses of Scripture in the formation of doctrine;
(b) the uses of historical statements to define our present faith: whether

verbal conformity is necessary or whether coherence of meaning is sufficient for agreement in faith;

(c) the process of response to, and reception of, ecumenical texts in faith and life, and to reflect upon those steps already taken in implementing the degree of agreement in faith already reached.

Resolution 10 - Anglican Centre in Rome

Resolved, that this Joint Meeting of the Primates of the Anglican Communion and the Anglican Consultative Council while regretting that it is not able to contribute to the Financial Appeal of the Anglican Centre in Rome from the core budget, encourages initiatives undertaken in the Provinces in support of the Appeal.

Resolution 11 - Week of Prayer for Christian Unity

Resolved, that this Joint Meeting of the Primates of the Anglican Communion and the Anglican Consultative Council notes with regret the many different times during the year at which the Week of Prayer is observed and recommends that the Faith and Order Commission of the World Council of Churches be requested to examine current practice with a view to establishing a common observance throughout the world.

Resolution 12 - Churches of Bangladesh, India and Pakistan

Resolved, that this Joint Meeting of the Primates of the Anglican Communion and the Anglican Consultative Council, recognising the mature experience of the Churches of Bangladesh, India and Pakistan in the development of full communion between Christians of different traditions, recommends that efforts be made to encourage deeper engagement of those Churches in the Ecumenical Advisory Group and the Inter-Anglican Theological and Doctrinal Consultation.

Resolution 13 - Date of Easter

Resolved, that this Joint Meeting of the Primates of the Anglican

Communion and the Anglican Consultative Council in the light of experience in Europe and throughout the world where Christians of both Eastern and Western traditions live and work together, and for our common witness, recommends that the Churches of East and West continue their efforts to establish a common date for the celebration of Easter.

Resolution 14 - Episcopal Authority and Oversight

Resolved, that this Joint Meeting of the Primates of the Anglican Communion and the Anglican Consultative Council, having received and considered communications from the International Bishops' Conference on Faith and Order and from the Episcopal Synod of America,

1. *Notes*:

    (a) the concern expressed in both letters about the future of those Anglicans who find themselves in minority situations in provinces which have accepted the ordination of women to the priesthood, and in some cases to the episcopate;

    (b) the suggestion of some form of ecclesial community which will enable such people 'to remain true to the historic faith and practice as expressed in our Anglican heritage'.

2. *Reaffirms* the continuing place in the Anglican Communion both of those who oppose and those who accept the ordination of women.

3. *Commits itself* to maintaining the highest level of communion within the Anglican Communion in the future.

Furthermore this meeting believes that this will be best achieved by reaffirming Resolution 72 of the Lambeth Conference, 1988, *viz.*,

'This conference:

    (1) Reaffirms its unity in the historical position of respect for diocesan boundaries and the authority of bishops within these boundaries; and in the light of the above.

    (2) Affirms that it is deemed inappropriate behaviour for any bishop or priest of this Communion to exercise episcopal or pastoral ministry within a diocese without first obtaining the permission and invitation of the ecclesial authority thereof.'

Resolutions of the Joint Meeting

4. *Calls upon* the bishops of the Anglican Communion to be scrupulously fair in the exercise of pastoral care to those who oppose and those who accept the ordination of women, particularly to those who are in minority situations, while always preserving the integrity of the faith and order of the Church.
5. *Welcomes* the elaboration of Lambeth Resolution 72 of 1988 in the Report of the Archbishop of Canterbury's Commission on Women in the Episcopate 1989 (the Eames Report), whose guidelines were endorsed by the Primates at Larnaca, Cyprus, 1989, and encourages each province to consider how the principles expressed in these documents may best be applied in its own circumstances.
6. *Requests* the Archbishop of Canterbury to re-convene the Eames Commission to consider further the theological and pastoral implications of the current situation within the Anglican Communion.

Resolution 15 - Revised Common Lectionary

Resolved, that this Joint Meeting of the Primates of the Anglican Communion and the Anglican Consultative Council:

Welcomes the publication of the Revised Common Lectionary (1992), which is now offered for use throughout the world, as a notable forward in ecumenical liturgical co-operation, and

Commends it to the Provinces and Member Churches of the Anglican Communion for study, testing, and consideration of its use, and for evaluation to be reported to the Co-ordinator for Liturgy.

Resolution 16 - Advisory Body on Prayer Books

Resolved, that this Joint Meeting of the Primates of the Anglican Communion and the Anglican Consultative Council, in reference to Resolution 18 of the Lambeth Conference 1988 (requesting the appointment of an Advisory Body on Prayer Books of the Anglican Communion),

> endorses the general recommendation made in the Report of the Co-ordinator for Liturgy and in particular the recommendation that the various Conferences, Councils, and Provinces of the Anglican Communion recognise and use these Consultations as the appropriate channels through which liturgical issues can be discussed and liturgical

norms discerned; and

Requests the Co-ordinator for Liturgy to facilitate work in this area.

Resolution 17 - Liturgical Revision

Resolved, that this Joint Meeting of the Primates of the Anglican Communion and the Anglican Consultative Council recognises the need for clear educational materials to facilitate understanding of continuity elements of liturgy described by Resolution 18 of the Lambeth Conference and Section 3.2 of Appendix A of the Report of the Co-ordinator for Liturgy ('An Advisory Body on Prayer Book Revision: A Statement on Behalf of the International Anglican Liturgical Consultation'), *viz.*:

> the public reading the Scriptures in a language understood by the people and instruction established on them;
>
> the use of the two dominical sacraments (baptism with water on the threefold Name and Holy Communion with bread and wine in intentional obedience to our Lord's command);
>
> episcopal ordination to each of the three orders by prayer with the laying-on of hands;
>
> the public recitation and teaching of the Apostles' and Nicene Creeds;
>
> and
>
> the use of other liturgical expressions of unity in faith and life which nurture the people of God and reflect awareness of ecumenical liturgical developments.

Resolution 18 - Christian Initiation

Resolved, that this Joint Meeting of the Primates of the Anglican Communion and the Anglican Consultative Council, urges the Provinces and Member Churches of the Anglican Communion to study and reflect on 'Walk in Newness of Life,' the statement on initiation of the 1991 International Anglican Liturgical Consultation, with a view to further discussion of the issues it has raised at a future meeting of the Primates and the Anglican Consultative Council.

Resolution 19 - Filioque Clause

Resolved, that this Joint Meeting of the Primates of the Anglican Communion and the Anglican Consultative Council, urges the Provinces and Member Churches of the Anglican Communion to respond to the requests of the 1978 and 1988 Lambeth Conferences, ACC-4, and ACC-8, that, in the words of Lambeth 1988, 'in future liturgical revisions the Niceno-Constantinopolitan Creed be printed without the Filioque clause', and to inform the Office of the Anglican Communion of their action.

Resolution 20 - Translation of Study Documents

Resolved, that this Joint Meeting of the Primates of the Anglican Communion and the Anglican Consultative Council, welcomes the provision made in the budget for translation of documents distributed for study into the languages of the Communion and requests the Secretary General to explore ways in which translation may be encouraged.

Resolution 21 - Calendar Revision

Resolved, that this Joint Meeting of the Primates of the Anglican Communion and the Anglican Consultative Council, adopts the following principles, criteria, and process for the recognition of men and women who have lived godly lives by including them in the calendars of the Churches for remembrance, having in mind that the revision of calendars is an ongoing process which is one of the ways in which the Church holds the Christian hope before the people of God, to enable their growth as a holy temple in the Lord (Eph. 2.21).

PRINCIPLES AND CRITERIA

The following principles and criteria are suggested:

a. The commemoration of holy people is always an act of anamnesis. We remember not only the person's historical events but the power of grace in their lives and consequently of 'Christ in us the hope of glory'. A calendar is an instrument for worship, just as much as a eucharistic prayer. We may learn from both, but we use them primarily for worship.

b. In worship, the practice of devotion (cult) precedes law. Law exists to protect cult from deformity, not to shape it. The first step in a process of commemoration is the spontaneous devotion of people who knew the person involved and testify to his/her holiness. Authority enters the process to encourage or discourage its continuation. (One of the ways in which the cult emerges is in the naming of churches and chapels after people who were known for their holiness of life, e.g., the John Keble Church in Mill Hill, London. The role of authority in such cases is to make sure that the criteria for this practice is holiness and witness and not power or wealth.)
c. Calendars should be developed to honour and expand the thankful remembering of Christian people. They should not be developed to meet pedagogical, regional, or sectionalist goals. The names of Christian heroes and heroines, however holy, should not be imposed onto the worship of people to whom they mean nothing.
d. A lean calendar may have more meaning and greater impact than a full calendar.
e. A process for trimming calendars may be as important as a process for developing them.
f. Originally, the word 'martyr' meant simply 'witness', but it was attached at an early date to those who persevered as witnesses to the point of death and whose death was itself the ultimate act of witness. The concept of martyrdom has become more complex in the intervening centuries. Is it to be restricted to those who might have avoided death but chose to remain firm in their resolve? Does it include those who were killed for their faith without the option of escape? Are only those who were killed by persecutors who were hostile to Christianity as such to be accounted martyrs (some provinces in the Communion have so ruled), or does martyrdom include those who have suffered at the hands of other Christians, perhaps for their doctrinal position or for their engagement with social evil?

   In societies which are nominally Christian it may be necessary to define martyrdom to include the killing of Christians by Christians. It is more than possible that those who were responsible, directly or indirectly, for the murder of Martin Luther King, Jr. and Oscar Romero, to name but two, were not only technically Christian (i.e. baptized) but acted on the basis of values which they misguidedly perceived to be Christian. The question is not who killed these witnesses, but whether they died for the authentic Gospel.
g. Some calendars restrict the word 'saint' to pre-Reformation figures; others do not. Anglicans should be neither intimidated nor beguiled by the technical terminology used traditionally and by Christians of other

Communions in regard to the commemoration of holy people and heroes and heroines of the faith. The word 'saint' means only 'holy person' and should not be used as though it separated a loved and respected Christian from the ordinary levels of humanity. The use of the term is optional.

Similarly, the word 'canonised' should not be used as though it implied human knowledge of divine judgement. There is, in fact, no compelling reason for Anglicans to appropriate the term, although it has been proposed in at least one province. A process of recognition after the cult has begun and historical statements have been attested will be valuable and may be called 'canonisation', but the term should not be used as though people become saints as a result of such a process; they become saints, if at all, through holiness of life and witness to the Gospel.

h. While commemorations begin at the local level, among those who knew and remember a holy person, it is not inappropriate for them to spread more widely, especially if the style of holiness expressed in the life of a person addresses in a striking way the aspirations of a particular generation of Christians. The love and courage of some people makes an almost universal appeal as their story becomes known. In such cases the boundaries of geography and of divided Christianity make little sense. It is not surprising that some Anglican calendars contain the names of people who lived in other parts of the world or belonged to other Christian Communions.

i. Reports of extraordinary phenomena (miracles, appearances) in association with a cult are not to be equated with evidence of holiness of life and witness to the gospel. They should be treated with caution, and not encouraged among those who may wish to promote a commemoration.

j. The following traits will be found in those who are commemorated.

  i. *Heroic faith*, i.e. bearing witness with great generosity to Christ and the gospel. Historically, the primary model of heroic faith has been witness to death, but the term may also include persistent risk-taking as well as a life in which other values are set aside for the sake of devotion and service. True heroic faith is healthy and life-affirming; it is not masochistic or suicidal.

  ii. *The fruit of the Spirit*. We may expect those commemorated to have exhibited in an exemplary way the fruit of the Spirit to which Paul refers in Gal. 5.22, 'love, joy, peace, patience, kindness, generosity, faithfulness, gentleness, and self-control'. Their lives may not have been perfect, but those who knew them should have been aware of this complex but unified goal within them.

  iii. *Christian engagement*. We may expect those who are commemo-

rated to have participation actively in the life of the Christian community and to have contributed to its sense of mission and to its life and growth.
iv. *Recognition by the Christian Community.* The commemoration of holy people should have spontaneous roots and should grow from the testimony of those who knew them. The task of authority is to prevent the spread of inappropriate or misleading devotion, not to impose a commemoration which promotes a line of thought or boosts regional self-esteem. The larger church is not obliged to approve such recognition as local Christian communities may give to particular people; however, it should take them seriously.

Process

Each Province should develop its own process for the liturgical commemoration of holy people. The process should include the following.

a. A climate in the church which is hospitable to local commemorations.
b. Recognition by bishops and other church leaders that they have a responsibility to review local commemorations and to encourage or discourage them as they appear (or do not appear) to foster devotion and holiness.
c. Provision for dioceses to suggest the names of people commemorated locally to an appropriate body of the Province for review (e.g., a Liturgical Commission or a sub-committee of a Liturgical Commission).
d. Provision for a body of the Province to test the acceptance of commemorations with a larger representation of the church.
e. Provision for the governing body of the Province to adopt names to be included in the provincial calendar, to assign them to a particular proper prayers and readings.
f. Support for the preparation and publication of accurate biographical material on those who are commemorated.
g. A process for the regular review of provincial calendars and for the 'retiring' of names which no longer command significant attention. (This should be done by the same provincial body which receives and reviews suggested names and tests their acceptance with the church, and in the same consultative way.)
h. A process for sharing calendar revision among the Provinces of the Communion.
i. Commitment to protecting Sundays as the weekly commemoration of

Resolutions of the Joint Meeting

the Lord, as well as the integrity of the great feasts and seasons. (If a holy person died on Christmas Day, for instance, it may be appropriate to commemorate him/her on his/her birthday or on the date of some other significant event in his/her life.)

j. Commitment to the commemoration of persons whose witness provides models for Christian life in the present context.

Resolution 22 - Co-ordinator of Liturgy and International Anglican Liturgy Consultation

Resolved, that this Joint Meeting of the Primates of the Anglican Communion and the Anglican Consultative Council commends the work of the Revd Paul Gibson, Co-ordinator of Liturgy, and endorses his continued co-operation with the International Anglican Liturgical Consultation, and be it further

Resolved, that this Meeting encourages the Provinces to respond positively to appeals for financial assistance to further the work of the International Anglican Liturgical Consultation.

Resolution 23 - Network for Inter-Faith Concerns

Resolved, that this Joint Meeting of the Primates of the Anglican Communion and the Anglican Consultative Council establishes a network of correspondents throughout the Anglican Communion, at no cost to the core budget, for Inter-Faith Concerns as mandated by Resolutions 20 and 21 of the 1988 Lambeth Conference, and be it further

Resolved, that the Network functions in accordance with the Guidelines for Anglican Consultative Council Networks agreed at the Anglican Consultative Council Standing Committee in 1988, and be it further

Resolved, that the Revd Nigel Pounde be appointed as the Convenor of the Network for a period of three years, responsible to the Standing Committee of the Anglican Consultative Council, and be it further

Resolved, that the Joint Standing Committee of Primates and Anglican Consultative Council nominate no fewer than three nor more than five persons to draw up terms of reference for the Network and to act as an advisory group for an initial period of three years.

Resolution 24 - Inter-Anglican Theological and Doctrinal Commission

Resolved, that this Joint Meeting of the Primates of the Anglican Communion and the Anglican Consultative Council:

1. Affirms the fine work of the Inter-Anglican Theological and Doctrinal Consultation, and receives its 1992 Report, *Belonging Together*. It commends the report to the provinces and dioceses for 'comment, creative critique, and expansion', as requested by the consultation.
2. Requests the Archbishop of Canterbury to thank the Consultation for its work, and the Virginia Theological Seminary for its generosity, and asks him to appoint a new representative Inter-Anglican Theological and Doctrinal Commission, possibly with a membership of about twelve to be accountable to the Archbishop of Canterbury and the Anglican Consultative Council.
3. Suggests that a date be set for reception of comments on *Belonging Together* from the Provinces, and that the new Commission continue the work begun by the Consultation in the light of comments from the Provinces, and that it report to the next meeting of the Anglican Consultative Council.

Resolution 25 - The Palestinian Deportees and the Middle East Peace Process

Resolved, that this Joint Meeting of the Primates of the Anglican Communion and the Anglican Consultative Council calls on the Israeli Government to comply immediately with United Nations Resolution 799, returning Palestinian deportees to their homes in the West Bank and Gaza; and be it further

Resolved, that the United Nations and member nations thereof enforce Resolution 799 and other resolutions having to do with the Israeli occupation of the West Bank and Gaza with the same rigour as is being applied against Iraq; and be it further

Resolutions of the Joint Meeting

Resolved, that this Meeting encourages the peace talks between Israel and the Palestinians and also the talks between Israel and the Vatican. It also urges the inclusion of the local indigenous Christians in all discussions on the future of Jerusalem, the position of Christians, and the holy places of that city; and be it finally

Resolved, that this Resolution be shared with the United Nations by the Anglican Observer; with the Governments of Israel, Palestine, Syria, Lebanon, Jordan and the Vatican by the President Bishop of the Episcopal Church in Jerusalem and the Middle East; and with the Government of the United States by the Presiding Bishop of the Episcopal Church in the United States of America; and that other members of the Joint Meeting of the Primates of the Anglican Communion and the Anglican Consultative Council be urged to encourage their governments to do likewise.

Explanation

At its May meeting in Amman, Jordan, the Anglican Refugee and Migrant Network called on Anglican Churches throughout the world to use their influence with their respective national governments to eradicate conditions creating refugees. The Amman meeting suggested a Day of Observance for Refugees during Epiphany, when the Holy Family was forced into flight into Egypt.

Meeting during Epiphany 1993 in Cape Town, the members of this Joint Meeting raised their voices on behalf of the many thousands of refugees, homeless and displaced persons of the world, and particularly on behalf of the 417 Palestinians recently deported from their homes by the Israeli Government and forced to subsist in a barren no-man's land.

We believe that resolutions of the United Nations should be enforced consistently. As they are now being enforced against Iraq, so should they be enforced against Israel, which by its act of deportation has violated both international law and the provisions of Resolution 799. The Resolution is clear and unequivocal: return the deportees to their homes.

We continue to pray for and support the peace process now underway among Israelis, Palestinians and their Arab neighbours. We welcome recent action of the Israeli Parliament to permit direct contact with the Palestine Liberation Organisation. We are grateful for the efforts of the President Bishop of the Episcopal Church in Jerusalem and the Middle East in promoting equally peace for Israel and Palestine. We urge that local, indigenous Christians of Jerusalem not be by-passed or absented from discussions on the future of Jerusalem, the holy places and, above all, on the living, indigenous Christian communities of the land. Their unique voices are essential to a just and peaceful future and must be heard.

Resolution 26 - Bosnia-Herzegovina

Resolved, that this Joint Meeting of the Primates of the Anglican Communion and the Anglican Consultative Council expresses its anguish and deep sorrow over the violent conflict in Bosnia-Herzegovina and adjacent territories of the former Yugoslavia, especially the apparently deliberate policies of mass rape of Muslim women and other abhorrent acts of 'ethnic cleansing'; and be it further

Resolved, that the definition of war crimes, the evidence of which in Bosnia-Herzegovina is already being gathered by the world community, be broadened to include rape as a weapon of war; and be it further

Resolved, that the United Nations and the European Community find ways and means to secure a political solution to the conflict and assure free access of humanitarian organisations to minister to the needs of the wounded, prisoners, refugees and displaced peoples in the region; and be it further

Resolved, that members of the Anglican Communion pray unceasingly and support wholeheartedly all local efforts for peace and reconciliation in this and other situations of violent conflict, taking special note of the global repercussions of ethnic and religious intolerance and hatred; and be it finally

Resolved, that this Resolution be shared with the United Nations and the European Community by the Anglican Observer to the United Nations.

Explanation

Compounding the inhumanity of the events of the last months in the former Yugoslavia, the savage rape of thousands of women in Bosnia happens as we carry on with our ordinary tasks in a presumably civilised world. Though the horror of it stretches our credulity, we know it is a reality for women from girlhood through old age. The most intimately violating of crimes is being used to terrorise and demoralise a people. These women and their families must have the prayers of the faithful everywhere, and our firm intention to work with every means at hand to end this horror and all other acts of 'ethnic cleansing', which inflame religious and ethnic prejudice and promote hatred instead of the peace at the heart of all true religion.

Resolution 27 - HIV/AIDS Education and Prevention

Resolved, that this Joint Meeting of the Primates of the Anglican Communion and the Anglican Consultative Council having considered the world-wide HIV/AIDS pandemic that is acute in many countries of the world, is moved with deep concern and compassion for those infected with the HIV virus, those suffering from AIDS, and their families, especially the orphaned children.

Notes with sorrow and regret that some governments are not admitting the extent of this disease; urges them to disclose the facts regarding HIV/AIDS in their respective countries as a first step towards developing the measures and means necessary to deal with this disease.

Endorses and supports the work of HIV/AIDS education and prevention throughout the Anglican Communion and urges the encouragement, strengthening and expansion of existing HIV/AIDS education and prevention programmes.

Urges all governments, all Churches, and all religious bodies to do all in their power to fight this killer of people.

Commends the Province of the Church of Uganda on its comprehensive programme of HIV/AIDS education and prevention developed in co-operation with ECUSA, the United States Agency for International Development and agencies of the United Nations, under the title of Church Human Services – Uganda; endorses this model of international partnership and commends it to other Provinces of the Anglican Communion; expresses appreciation for the willingness of the Church of Uganda to respond to requests from other Provinces for technical assistance in developing programmes to combat HIV/AIDS in their own countries.

Resolution 28 - Development and Deployment of Nuclear Weapons

Resolved, that this Joint Meeting of the Primates of the Anglican Communion and the Anglican Consultative Council calls upon the Churches of the Anglican Communion to support any initiatives to seek an advisory opinion from the International Court of Justice as to whether the development and deployment of nuclear weapons and the threat to use them are legal under existing international law, and further

Resolved, that the text of this resolution be conveyed to the Secretary General of the United Nations and that the Provinces be requested to convey their responses to the Anglican Communion Office and to the Anglican Observer at the United Nations.

Resolution 29 - Sudan

1. Resolved, that this Joint Meeting of the Primates of the Anglican Communion and the Anglican Consultative Council, urges Member Churches to do everything in their power to draw the attention of their nations to the tragedy in the Sudan, particularly in its religious dimension, and further
2. Urges the All-Africa Conference of Churches to seek the resolution of the crisis in the Sudan in co-operation with the Organisation of African Unity, and further
3. Commends the Episcopal Church of Sudan for bringing to an end the schism which has existed for six years. The Primates and members of the Anglican Consultative Council are convinced that the Unity of the Church in the Sudan is essential in the process of bringing peace and reconciliation in the country and further
4. Expresses solidarity with and prayerful concern for the life of the Episcopal Church of Sudan and the people of that country and finally
5. Encourages the Provinces of the Anglican Communion to do all in their power to help the Episcopal Church of the Sudan materially.

Resolution 30 - Cyprus

Resolved, that this Joint Meeting of the Primates of the Anglican Communion and the Anglican Consultative Council, having in mind the many United Nations Resolutions since 1974 concerning the Turkish invasion of the Island of Cyprus and especially that the Turkish Government should withdraw its troops from the Island, this Joint Meeting of the Primates of the Anglican Communion and the Anglican Consultative Council re-affirms its belief in the rule of law and the unity of the Island of Cyprus and the authority of the United Nations and asks that the United Nations Resolutions on Cyprus be implemented as soon as possible.

Resolution 31 - Nuclear Wastes

Resolved, that this Joint Meeting of the Primates of the Anglican Communion and the Anglican Consultative Council, noting that the people of the South Pacific face the economic and ecological ravages of the dan-

Resolutions of the Joint Meeting

gers in dumping wastes and poisonous gases and that a similar resolution of the Anglican Consultative Council in 1990 had apparently achieved no result, asks the Anglican Observer at the United Nations to convey to the Secretary General of the UN our concern for an immediate end to these practices.

Resolution 32 - Bougainville

Resolved, that this Joint Meeting of the Primates of the Anglican Communion and the Anglican Consultative Council, endorses the statement released by the Anglican bishops of the South Pacific Anglican Council on the situation on the island of Bougainville in Papua New Guinea and assures the people of Bougainville and their government of its prayers.

South Pacific Anglican Bishops Statement on Bougainville

As Bishops from Anglican Dioceses in Papua New Guinea, the Solomon Islands, Vanuatu and Polynesia, we have met together and discussed the situation on Bougainville. We recognise that the conflict there is a complex issue and the result of many different factors.

However, at the present time innocent people are suffering from the absence of stable government and the lack of essential services such as health and education. In order that help can be given to people who have now been the victims of war for a number of years, we make the following appeals:

1. We appeal to the Bougainville Revolutionary Army to lay down their arms and immediately accept the restoration of government services.
2. We appeal to the Papua New Guinea government to speed up the work of sending relief to Bougainville and to invite independent observers from either the Commonwealth or the South Pacific Forum to be present in the island and report on human rights violations. At the same time, we wish to commend the Papua New Guinea government for its decision to involve the churches, through the Papua New Guinea Council of Churches in the restoration of essential services to Bougainville.
3. We appeal to all sides to accept, that for the present, Bougainville must be regarded as an integral part of Papua New Guinea but we also urge that peaceful dialogue about the political future of the island continue through democratic channels.

Therefore, we Bishops of the South Pacific Anglican Church meeting in the Solomon Islands pray fervently that 'the sound of weeping and of crying will be heard no more . . . but peace and harmony may reign, and the wolf and the lamb will feed together' as children of God (Isa. 65.19, 25).

Resolution 33 - Haiti

Resolved, that this Joint Meeting of the Primates of the Anglican Communion and the Anglican Consultative Council, bearing in mind the continued unrest and the suspension of civil order in Haiti and regretting the suffering and hardship being experienced by the people of that country:

1. Urges that a democratically elected government be restored to Haiti as soon as possible, and
2. Requests the United States Administration to adopt a compassionate attitude towards Haitian refugees, and
3. Asks the Peace and Justice Network and the Anglican Observer to the United Nations to monitor the situation and through the Anglican Communion Secretariat support appropriate actions that will give expression to the sentiments of this Resolution.

Resolution 34 - Peacemaking and Demilitarisation

Resolved, that this Joint Meeting of the Primates of the Anglican Communion and the Anglican Consultative Council expresses its profound hope for the success of two peace processes now underway on behalf of peace in the Philippines and the Middle East, and further hopes for the successful implementation of the peace agreement in El Salvador.

Urgently calls upon our Member Churches throughout the world to support our partner Province, the Philippine Episcopal Church, as it encourages a peace process to bring about a just peace to the 23-year-old conflict in that country. We affirm the efforts of the Peace and Justice Network in assisting parties as they seek to come together to reconcile the root causes of the conflict.

Resolution 35 - Debt and Sustainable Development

Resolved, that this Joint meeting of the Primates of the Anglican Communion and the Anglican Consultative Council, recognising the terrible consequences of the debt burden, especially among the third world countries, recommends that the Anglican Peace and Justice Network and the United Nations Observer create a Debt and Alternative Development Working Group for addressing the burden placed on poor people through foreign debt which undermines genuine development; and the following strategies be implemented, and that the following statement be issued:

1. We encourage actions by churches and people's organisations to take all peaceful steps to place pressure on governments to eliminate or reduce the burden of debt;
2. We encourage the development of alternative models of sustainable development based on local ownership and appropriate technology.
3. We are encouraged to join with leaders of other churches in meeting with their governments and diplomatic representatives of other countries to initiate discussions of multilateral, as opposed to bilateral, debt negotiations, and to publicise such activity.

Further recommends that the next Lambeth Conference place the issue of debt and development on its agenda.

Resolution 36 - Democracy and Empowerment

Resolved, that this Joint Meeting of the Primates of the Anglican Communion and the Anglican Consultative Council encourages Provinces and partner Churches of the Anglican Communion to be active in working towards the creation of a substantive, participatory democracy in those countries where it is at present only a formal structure or non-existent:

1. The Communion as a whole supports the efforts of those provinces and partner churches engaged in the struggle for genuine democracy.
2. That every Province and partner Church engage in community development work and develop resources for this task.
3. That every Province, and partner Church examine its own structures, to enable people to participate more fully in decision-making processes.

Resolution 37 - Sexual Abuse

Resolved, that this Joint Meeting of the Primates of the Anglican Communion and the Anglican Consultative Council urges all Provinces to work to end sexual abuse and exploitation of women and children throughout the Anglican Church, and calls on congregations to provide pastoral care to victims of sexual abuse and exploitation; and further expresses its shame that there is evidence of cases of sexual abuse within the Anglican Church and calls on congregations to provide pastoral care to victims of sexual abuse and further condemns commercial practices of sexual exploitation, such as 'mail order brides' and child prostitution.

Resolution 38 - Women's Encounter

Resolved, that this Joint meeting of the Primates of the Anglican Communion and the Anglican Consultative Council notes the Report of the participants in the Anglican Encounter: A Celebration of Hope, 1992 and draws to its attention the opening paragraphs

> At this midpoint of the Ecumenical Decade of Churches in Solidarity with Women, we challenge the church to take the Decade more seriously, and to recognise that the Decade is not just about women's participation in the church, but is about solidarity with all women in all aspects of their lives.
> We challenge the church to commit its resources (of money, personnel and attention) to supporting the aims of the Decade.
> We call upon the church to affirm the alternative economic, political and relational models that women are offering to the world.

Resolution 39 - Refugee and Migration Network

Resolved, that the Joint Meeting of the Primates of the Anglican Communion and the Anglican Consultative Council affirms the value of an on-going Anglican Refugee and Migration Network and requests the Joint Standing Committees of the Primates and the Anglican Consultative Council to include in the Inter-Anglican budget as a priority from January 1993 sufficient funds and staff time to resource a quarterly information newsletter among members of the Refugee and Migration Network.

Resolution 40 - Youth

Resolved, that this Joint Meeting of the Primates of the Anglican Communion and the Anglican Consultative Council:

1. Strongly affirms the value and place of young people within the life of the Anglican Communion and regrets the cancellation of the International Conference of Young Anglicans, and

The Church of today – a young pilgrim at Canterbury

2. That the Inter-Anglican Youth Network be re-activated by asking the Provinces, who have committed money to the Youth Conference but which has not yet been spent, to enable a meeting of a group of key people and the launch of the network, and
3. Encourages and supports the programming of an International Conference of Young Anglicans at an appropriate time as determined by the next meeting of the Standing Committee of the Anglican Consultative Council, and
4. That all Provinces of the Communion be invited to contribute towards a central fund for the event.

Resolution 41 - Anglican Observer at the United Nations

Resolved, that the Joint Meeting of the Primates of the Anglican Communion and the Anglican Consultative Council receives with pleasure the Report of the Anglican Observer at the United Nations and acknowledges:

a. the significant achievements of this office to date;
b. the commitment of the Anglican Communion to the United Nations implicit in this office, and in Resolution 24 of ACC-8;
c. the increasing importance of the United Nations and its agencies as a global forum for Peace and Justice;
d. the potential for effective linking with Anglican networks and structures of the Communion which this office provides; and
   i. *Commends* the Report to Member Churches for information;
   ii. *Asks* Member Churches to keep the Office of the Anglican Observer at the United Nations informed of appropriate developments and resolutions;
   iii. *Recommends* that member Churches consider the feasibility of offering both prayerful and financial support to this office, and
   iv. *Urges* the Inter-Anglican Finance Committee to make a contribution to this office from the Inter-Anglican Budget as soon as possible.

Resolution 42 - International Aid Programmes

Resolved, that this Joint Meeting of the Primates of the Anglican Communion and the Anglican Consultative Council:

Resolutions of the Joint Meeting

1. encourages Provinces in 'donor' nations to challenge their governments about the levels, intentions and expectations of their aid programmes;
2. encourages Provinces in 'developing' nations to challenge their governments and churches about integrity with which aid is applied in their countries; and
3. encourages donor agencies to respect human dignity in their fund-raising appeals.

Resolution 43 - MISAG II

Resolved, that this Joint meeting of the Primates of the Anglican Communion and the Anglican Consultative Council, noting the excellent work done by MISAG II, as recorded in their final report, *Towards Dynamic Mission*, recommends:

a. that the MISAG II Report be translated into the major Regional languages of the Communion and commended in its entirety to the churches and theological institutions of the Communion for study and application, and more specifically;
b. that an Anglican Mission Commission, Missio, be established as outlined on pages 49-51 of the report, but with the additional function of exploring ways of developing theological perspectives for mission and evangelism for the Communion;
c. that Missio be charged with the responsibility of exploring the feasibility and modalities for 'Movement for Mission Conference' (Brisbane II); and to make recommendations to the Standing Committees of the Anglican Consultative Council and Primates;
d. That the original vision of Partners in Mission as an on-going process of mutuality and interdependence be recovered and re-emphasised in place of the current rather expensive and often burdensome one-off consultation approach. (MISAG II, pp. 24-29);
e. that a pastoral letter incorporating the vision, spirit, and salient concerns of this conference be written on behalf of the Primates and ACC-9, and signed by the Archbishop of Canterbury, translated into the major Regional languages of the Communion and circulated as soon as possible.

Resolution 44 - The Decade of Evangelism

Resolved, that this Joint Meeting of the Primates of the Anglican Communion and the Anglican Consultative Council, having noted from the reports of various provinces that the vision of the Decade of Evangelism has made, and will continue to make, an impact in the life and ministry of the Church throughout the Communion; and

That in those parts of the Communion where the vision is taken seriously; there is spectacular growth in the Church; recommends:

a. that provinces and regions be encouraged to organise consultations on evangelism, making use of resource people from around the Communion for teaching and training;

b. that a list of gifted resource persons be provided by the Anglican Consultative Council Secretariat to the Provinces indicating each person's area of expertise;

c. that the provision of video resources in appropriate languages be continued by the Secretariat, especially for helping local church leaders become more aware of what is happening outside their own locality in the Decade of Evangelism, and thus motivating them for action;

d. that a mid-point review of the Decade be made by seeking reports from the provinces in 1995, which should be evaluated by ACC-10 and Primates' Meeting in 1996, and followed by recommendations to the churches;

e. that the Provinces be encouraged to restore the Catechumenate, or discipling process, to help enquiries move to Christian faith, using the witness and support of lay people, and liturgically celebrating the stages of growth;

f. that provinces be encouraged to provide more resources for

- lay theological education
- ministry with children and youth
- equipping Christians for Evangelism within the Family;

g. that the Standing Committees of the Primates and the Anglican Consultative Council give consideration to planning for the year 2000, a significant Communion-wide celebration of the renewal of our commitment to mission and evangelism, and the beginning of a new century.

h. that Anglican Provinces be encouraged to co-operate with other churches in the Ministry of Evangelism where this is practical.

i. that Provinces challenge local churches, where necessary, to be more hospitable and welcoming to visitors and inquirers.

Resolution 45 - Peace Award

Resolved, that the Joint Meeting of the Primates of the Anglican Communion and the Anglican Consultative Council, noting the crying need for peace in the world, and the need to encourage people to work for peace and the exemplary involvement of Anglicans in peace and justice issues, recommends:

1. the initiation of an Anglican Peace Award to be presented to individuals or groups within the Anglican Communion who have shown outstanding commitment and involvement as peacemakers;
2. that the Joint Standing Committees of the Primates of the Anglican Consultative Council process the matter further, and
3. that the award be made by the Archbishop of Canterbury annually.

Resolution 46 - Spirituality

Resolved, that this Joint Meeting of the Primates of the Anglican Communion and the Anglican Consultative Council:

1. notes with approval the recovery of many of the great traditions of spirituality in recent years and recognises the encouraging growth of institutes of Christian spirituality and the retreat movement in our provinces;
2. commends the importance of attention to spiritual formation in the churches of the Anglican Communion; and
3. calls upon those involved in the spirituality movement throughout the Communion to create a loose network for mutual instruction and enrichment.

Resolution 47 - New Provinces of Burundi, Rwanda and Zaire

Resolved, that this Joint Meeting of the Primates and the Anglican Communion and the Anglican Consultative Council welcomes the creation of the Province of Burundi, the Province of Rwanda, and the Province of Zaire and requests the Primates to add them to the list of Member Churches of the Anglican Communion, and that they be added to the Schedule of Membership of the Anglican Consultative Council.

Resolution 48 - New Province of Korea

Resolved, that this Joint Meeting of the Primates of the Anglican Communion and the Anglican Consultative Council welcomes the progress towards the creation of the new Province of Korea in April 1993 and requests the Primates to add it to the list of member Churches of the Anglican Communion following its inauguration, and that it be added to the Schedule of Membership of the Anglican Consultative Council.

The Anglican Church of Korea – our newest province, the Most Revd Simon Kim, Primate

Resolution 49 - Inter-Anglican Information Network

Resolved, that this Joint Meeting of the Primates and the Anglican Communion and the Anglican Consultative Council:

1. re-affirms the usefulness of telecommunications in mission and ministry;
2. requests the Anglican Consultative Council to continue the operation and development of the Inter-Anglican Information Network (IAIN) as the principal communications service of the Anglican Communion by arranging with volunteers and contracted staff, as funds may allow, for the management of the IAIN system; by seeking project grant funding for its continuation and growth and by the creation of a task force of church related telecommunication specialists representing the diverse regions of the Communion to guide the on-going development of IAIN;
3. directs that the task force be accountable to the Anglican Consultative Council through its communications office and include, ex-officio, the Communications Officer and the Director of Administration and Finance; the cost of task-force meetings and its work 'on line' to be charged to the IAIN Project Budget and
4. requests the IAIN Task Force to prepare and implement a plan to inform all Anglican Communion Provincial, Diocesan and related offices about the availability and benefits of the IAIN Network with a view to encouraging increased participation.

Resolution 50 - Appreciation for Trinity Parish

Whereas, the initial consultations about the potential for telecommunications to be of service to the Anglican Communion were convened by the Parish of Trinity Church, New York City, and

Whereas, Trinity made possible the demonstration and use of the Inter-Anglican Information Network at the 1988 Lambeth Conference, and

Whereas, that parish has provided grants for the development of telecommunication staffing initially in one location and now, in three regions of the Communion, and

Whereas, it continues to make possible the demonstration and use of telecommunications at key international meetings of the Communion, and

Whereas, Trinity is helping leaders in provinces and dioceses in the global south begin the use of telecommunication in order to have more frequent and regular contact with others in their own region and throughout the Communion,

Resolved, that the Joint Meeting of the Primates of the Anglican Communion and the Anglican Consultative Council, expresses its deep gratitude to the Parish of Trinity Church, New York City, and its Trinity Grants Program and staff, for their foresight and commitment to assisting the Anglican Communion in the exploration and development of communication systems to serve the Communion. We acknowledge gratefully the substantial grants to the Anglican Consultative Council from Trinity Church which have made possible the creation of the Inter-Anglican Information Network in faithful response to a 1988 Lambeth Conference resolution asking that such a network be established.

Resolution 51 - Model of Representation in the Anglican Consultative Council

Resolved, that the Anglican Consultative Council, adopts the proposed model of representation set out below and directs that the constitution of the Anglican Consultative Council be amended accordingly.

Group 1.	Provinces over 1,000,000	1 bishop + 1 priest + 1 lay person
Group 2.	Provinces between 250,000 and 1 million	1 bishop or 1 priest + 1 lay person
Group 3.	Provinces less than 250,000	1 person (preferably lay)

Resolution 52 - Guidelines for Provincial Constitutions

Resolved, that this Joint Meeting of the Primates of the Anglican Communion and the Anglican Consultative Council, directs the addition of the following clause to the 'Guidelines for Provincial Constitutions and Metropolitical Authority' agreed to at ACC-4 (Resolution 16).

At the consecration of a Bishop, the Bishop should undertake canonical obedience in all things lawful to the Metropolitan and to the upholding of provincial and diocesan constitutions.

Resolution 53 - Cohabitation outside Marriage

Resolved, that this Joint Meeting of the Primates of the Anglican Communion and the Anglican Consultative Council refer the Report of Working Group III on co-habitation outside marriage to the Family Network for consideration and further work on this subject.

Resolution 54 - Irregular Episcopal Consecrations

Resolved, that this Joint Meeting of the Primates of the Anglican Communion and the Anglican Consultative Council, requests the Primates, when a threat of irregular episcopal consecration appears imminent, to review the situation and take such action as they deem appropriate.

Resolution 55 - Budget Priorities

Resolved, that this Joint Meeting of the Primates of the Anglican Communion and the Anglican Consultative Council, receives the report on priorities and budgets from Working Group III of this meeting and refers it along with a summary of points made in the discussion to the Joint Standing Committees for further study; and

that the Joint Standing Committees be authorised to take appropriate action; and

that the Joint Standing Committees be asked to report the results of the study and any actions taken to the next meetings of the Primates and the Anglican Consultative Council.

Resolution 56 - Contributions to the Inter-Anglican Budget

Resolved, that this Joint Meeting of the Primates of the Anglican Communion and the Anglican Consultative Council, recognising the failure of some Provinces to meet their financial quotas and the inevitable effect

this will have on weakening the infrastructure of our Communion calls on all Provinces to:
1. make this a matter of prayerful concern;
2. do all in their power to meet their quotas; and
3. secure other ways of ensuring that our Communion is not impaired by the financial consequences of failing to meet budgeted expenditure.

Resolution 57 - Inter-Anglican Budget for the Triennium 1994-96

Resolved, that this Joint Meeting of the Primates of the Anglican Communion and the Anglican Consultative Council approves the Budgets presented by the Inter-Anglican Finance Committee for the Triennium 1994-6 (see page 129/32) with the recommendation that the identification of priorities taken by the meeting be taken into account when the budget is reviewed.

Resolution 58 - Revised allocation of contributions to the Inter-Anglican Budget

Resolved, that this Joint Meeting of the Primates of the Anglican Communion and the Anglican Consultative Council accepts the revised allocation of contributions to the Inter-Anglican Budget as set out on page 133.

Resolution 59 - Appointment of Secretary General

Resolved, that the Anglican Consultative Council, authorises the Standing Committee to appoint for a specified term, with option for renewal, the next Secretary General on the advice of the Archbishop of Canterbury and the Selection Committee.

Resolution 60 - Charitable Trustees Incorporation Act 1872

Resolved, that whereas the coming into effect of the Charities Act 1992 abolishes the office of Official Custodian for Charities, the decision of the Standing Committee to incorporate the Anglican Consultative Council under the Charitable Trustees Incorporation Act 1872 is hereby endorsed, and they are empowered to take whatever steps are necessary to ensure this.

Resolution 61 - Common Seal

Resolved, consequent upon the incorporation of the Council under the Trustees Incorporation Act 1872 it is resolved that the following Bye-law be added to the Council's Constitution under powers given in Clause 2(0) of the Constitution, and the Bye-laws renumbered appropriately:

> The Seal of the Council shall not be affixed to any Instrument except by authority of a Resolution of the Standing Committee, and in the presence of the Secretary of the Standing Committee or the Chairman of the Standing Committee, and the said member shall sign every instrument to which the seal shall be so affixed in their presence the Seal to be at all times in the custody of the Secretary.

Resolution 62 - Inclusive Language

Resolved, that this Joint Meeting of the Primates of the Anglican Communion and the Anglican Consultative Council, urges the Joint Standing Committees of the Primates and the Anglican Consultative Council, to ensure that, as much as possible, gender-inclusive language is used in all future documents, presentations and acts of worship of the Anglican Consultative Council and Primates meetings.

Resolution 63 - ACC - 10

Resolved, that this Joint Meeting of the Primates of the Anglican Communion and the Anglican Consultative Council

1. welcomes the invitation from the Bishop of Panama to host ACC-10 and, if agreed, the meeting of the Primates of the Anglican Communion;
2. directs the Secretary General to make recommendations on the invitation and to report to the next meeting of the Standing Committees.

Resolution 64 - Secretary General

Whereas, the Revd Canon Dr Samuel Van Culin has served the Anglican Communion well and faithfully for more than a decade as the first Secretary General of the Anglican Consultative Council and more recently

Resolutions of the Joint Meeting

Canon Samuel Van Culin

as Secretary General of the Anglican Communion, and whereas, in both positions, he has been at the heart of the development of the Anglican Consultative Council, the Primates' Meeting, and the Lambeth Conference, and whereas, this will be the last meeting of both the Primates and the

Resolutions of the Joint Meeting

Anglican Consultative Council at which he will be acting as Secretary General, though serving until the end of 1994, now therefore be it

Resolved, that this Joint Meeting of the Primates of the Anglican Consultative Communion and the Anglican Consultative Council gives thanks to God for his many gifts, wisdom, character, devotion to his task, diplomacy, sensitivity to the diversity of the Communion, energies and supporting friendship and expresses a deep gratitude for his many contributions to the Anglican Communion and its individual members.

Resolution 65 - Southern Africa

Resolved, that this Joint Meeting of the Primates of the Anglican Communion and the Anglican Consultative Council give thanks to God for the encouraging developments that have occurred in Southern Africa in recent years.

We give particular thanks for the achievement by Namibians of their political independence and for the end of the devastating civil war in Mozambique. We salute the Right Revd Dinis Sengulane, a member of the Anglican Consultative Council, for his uncompromising stand against violence and for his role in helping to bring about peace. We give thanks for the announcement of elections in Lesotho. We pray for a return to multi-party democracy in that land and for movement towards free political activity and democracy in the Kingdom of Swaziland.

In South Africa we thank God for the movement, however slow and halting, towards a non-racial democracy. We pay tribute to the millions of South Africans who sacrificed so much to bring pressure on the minority government to change its course, and we acknowledge the courage of President F.W. de Klerk in finally responding to that pressure in February 1990, by lifting the ban on political organisations and freeing political prisoners such as Nelson Mandela. We share with our brothers and sisters in South Africa their frustration at the slow pace of constitutional talks. We identify with them in condemning the failure of the Government to act vigorously to end the violence which wracks the country. We are shocked that despite three years of talks about democracy there is scant evidence of any meaningful improvements to the lives of ordinary South Africans. We call on the country's political leaders not to play with the lives of people by tactics of clinging to power, of point-scoring, of grandstanding and brinkmanship. We call for the speedy introduction of interim arrangements for multi-party rule, pending elections for a constituent assembly to draw up a new constitution. We appeal to all parties to work for the holding of an election

Resolutions of the Joint Meeting

The Southern Africa delegation

during 1993 and we call for an end to the racist system of conscripting white South Africans for military service. On the issue of sanctions, we believe the international community should be guided by representatives of the victims of apartheid. We stand by Archbishop Tutu's call that sanctions be lifted only when the Government takes effective action to end the violence or there is multi-party control of the security forces.

We note that Anglican leaders in South Africa, led by the bishops of the Province, are putting all political leaders and parties under the critical scrutiny to which the Government was subjected in the days when many other parties were outlawed. We applaud this new development in the prophetic ministry of the South African church. We pledge our support to both our Province and other churches in South Africa when they speak out for the weak and the marginalised and against those who misuse power.

Finally, we would be ungrateful guests if we did not express heartfelt thanks to our host Province for the generous and unstinting hospitality they have shown to us, gathered from the four corners of the earth. Truly we have been received as sisters and brothers in Christ and for this we are grateful beyond words.

'We're not in the business of keeping the rumour of God alive. I'm not interested in rumours. But I am interested in promoting a full-blooded Christian faith that's rooted in the historic faith of the Church and yet is open to new truth, from whatever direction it comes.'

Archbishop George Carey.

Appendices

The Conference Hymn

O Christ the King of glory
who chose the way of loss,
to share the human story,
to bear the bitter cross;
by loving self-surrender,
by all the pains you bore,
you won for us the splendour
of life for evermore.

May God, whose care unsleeping
holds all beneath his hand,
enfold you in his keeping
the Church in every land.
Through doubtings and denials,
through grief and glory come,
through all the fiery trials
he leads his children home.

O Lord of life, ascended
to glory from the grave,
your grace shall be extended
to help and heal and save.
O Captain of salvation
in mercy bring to birth
your new redeemed creation
from all the pains of earth.

To God alone be blessing
and heartfelt ceaseless praise,
a love beyond expressing,
to everlasting days.
Proclaim salvation's story,
dominions, thrones and powers!
By cross and grave and glory
a living hope is ours.

Suggested tune: Aurelia 76.76. D

© The Rt Rev Timothy Dudley-Smith, July 1992. Written especially for the Cape Town meetings.

Sister Evodia, one of the many Religious in the Province of Southern Africa, visited the Cape Town meeting

Statement of Purpose

1. To identify and enter into each other's concerns and priorities through worship, group discussion and informal occasions.

2. To determine the priorities of the Inter-Anglican bodies for the years 1994, 1995 and 1996 in the light of financial resources.

3. To strengthen the Communion by considering a renewed vision of Anglican identity and the exercise of authority in the Communion.

4. To affirm our vocation in mission and evangelism and identify practical steps for communion-wide co-operation.

5. To nourish growth in communion with ecumenical partners at all levels and identify new initiatives.

The Plenary Hall banner

Appendices

6. To consult and advise the Archbishop of Canterbury concerning the date, style, membership and location of the next Lambeth Conference; and to identify the meetings leading to it.

7. To approve the job description and begin the process for appointing a new Secretary General.

8. To hear reports of the networks, the Church of the Province of Southern Africa and the regions, and to respond to urgent and topical issues.

Decisions at a Glance

CHRISTIAN UNITY

The Joint Meeting:
- re-affirmed commitment to Christian unity and to full Anglican participation in the World Council of Churches;
- acknowledged widespread Anglican disappointment at the Vatican's official response to ARCIC I, but nevertheless expressed gratitude for many signs of progress in relations between Anglicans and Roman Catholic at local level;
- encouraged the next Anglican/Oriental Orthodox Forum to work on a clear Christology statement;
- encouraged local dialogue with Baptist communities;
- urged member Churches to give practical assistance to the Orthodox Churches of Eastern Europe and the Commonwealth of Independent States;
- agreed to the creation of an Anglican/Old Catholic Co-ordinating Council to discuss theological issues and explore joint mission in Europe;
- welcomed recent agreements between Anglicans and Lutherans in Europe and the USA, and encouraged work towards full communion between Anglicans and the Nordic and Baltic Churches;
- called for study on the methodology used in ecumenical dialogue, particularly use of Scripture and the historic statements of participating Churches;
- encouraged initiatives taken by various Provinces to support the endowment appeal for the Anglican Centre in Rome;
- requested the Faith and Order Commission of the World Council of

Statement of Purpose

Churches to try to find a common time to observe the Week of Prayer for Christian Unity;
- welcomed deeper engagement of the united Churches of Bangladesh, North India, Pakistan and South India in bodies such as the Ecumenical Advisory Group and the Inter-Anglican Theological and Doctrinal Commission;
- indicated Anglican support of discussions between the Eastern and Western Churches seeking a common date for Easter;

THE DYNAMICS OF COMMUNION AND LITURGY

The Meeting:
- re-affirmed the continuing place in Anglicanism of those for and against the ordination of women, called on bishops to be scrupulously fair in their pastoral care of those unable to accept the ordination of women as priests, and sought the re-convening of the Eames Commission;
- welcomed publication of the Revised Common Lectionary (1992) and encouraged Provinces to consider its use;
- recognised the need for simple educational material to explain the basic shape of Anglican liturgical worship;
- commended *Walk in Newness of Life*, International Liturgical Consultation's statement on initiation, for study and comment;
- encouraged Provinces involved in Liturgical revision to consider omitting the Filioque Clause from the Nicene Creed;
- encouraged wider use of translation for Inter-Anglican documents;
- adopted a set of principles for recognition of godly people who could be included in future Church calendars;
- commended the work of the Revd Paul Gibson, Co-ordinator for Liturgy, and encouraged Provinces to support financially the work of the International Anglican Liturgical Consultation;
- commended *Belonging Together* the report of the Inter-Anglican Theological and Doctrinal Consultation, thanked the Virginia Theological Seminary (USA) for its generous support of the Consultation, and asked the Archbishop of Canterbury to set up a permanent Inter-Anglican Theological and Doctrinal Commission.

TOPICAL CONCERNS

The Meeting:
- expressed humanitarian concern about the plight of deportees from Gaza and the West Bank by Israel;

Appendices

- expressed 'anguish and deep sorrow' over conflict in the former Yugoslavia;
- expressed support for the work of HIV/AIDS education and prevention and urged governments to disclose fully the extent of AIDS infection within their borders;
- called for Church support for initiatives to obtain an opinion from the International Court of Justice as to whether the deployment of nuclear weapons or the threat to use them is legal;
- asked Provinces to draw attention to the tragedy of civil war in the Sudan, sought help of the All-African Conference of Churches and the Organisation of African Unity in the quest for peace, and expressed thanks for the end of the six-year schism in the life of the Episcopal Church of Sudan;
- re-affirmed belief in the unity of the island of Cyprus and called on Turkey to withdraw its troops and comply with the relevant United Nations resolutions;
- expressed concern about continued dumping of nuclear waste in the South Pacific region;
- supported calls for a negotiated peace in Bougainville, Papua New Guinea;
- expressed concern about the civil unrest and the suspension of civil order in Haiti;
- expressed hope for the success of the peace processes now underway in the Philippines, the Middle East and El Salvador;
- called for more action to alleviate the growing problem of debt, particularly in the third world;
- Urged all Provinces to work to end sexual abuse and the exploitation of women and children, and urged congregations to take more initiatives in their pastoral care.

NETWORK CONCERNS

The Meeting:
- drew attention to the call by participants in the Anglican Encounter 1992, for the Churches to take more seriously the Ecumenical Decade of Churches in Solidarity with Women;
- affirmed the value of an on-going Refugee and Migration Network, and the Youth Network;
- welcomed the achievements so far of the Anglican Observer at the United Nations, and encouraged financial support for the work by Member Churches;

Statement of Purpose

- encouraged Provinces in 'donor' nations to challenge their governments about their levels of aid programmes, and Provinces in 'receiver' nations to challenge their governments and churches to apply aid received with integrity.

EVANGELISM AND MISSION POLICY

The Meeting:
- supported the establishment of a Mission Commission, to be called Missio, to co-ordinate mission policy and undertake theological reflection on mission issues;
- encouraged continued sharing of information and resources in the Decade of Evangelism;
- recommended the creation of an Anglican Peace Award, to be made annually by the Archbishop of Canterbury;
- encouraged creation of a network of those involved in promoting Christian Spirituality.

ANGLICAN COMMUNION CONCERNS

The Meeting:
- welcomed creation of new Provinces in Burundi, Rwanda and Zaire and asked the Primates to add them to the Schedule of Membership of the Anglican Communion. Welcomed inauguration of the Province of Korea in April 1993;
- re-affirmed the usefulness of telecommunications in mission and ministry and encouraged the continued development of the Inter-Anglican Information Network (IAIN);
- expressed thanks to Trinity Parish, New York, for its support of the Inter-Anglican Information Network (IAIN);
- reviewed the basis on which Provinces were represented on the Anglican Consultative Council;
- added a clause about the Canonical Obedience of Bishops to their Metropolitans to official guidelines for provincial and diocesan constitutions;
- referred the question of cohabitation outside marriage to the Family Network for study and advice;
- urged all Provinces to do all in their power to meet their share of the Inter-Anglican budget;
- approved the Inter-Anglican budget, and the list of allocations to Member Churches;

Appendices

- authorised the Joint Standing Committee to appoint the next Secretary General, on advice from the Archbishop of Canterbury and the selection committee;
- urged use of gender-inclusive language in Inter-Anglican documents, presentations and acts of worship;
- accepted the invitation of the Bishop of Panama to host ACC 10, and, if agreed, the Primates' Meeting;
- recorded its thanks to Canon Sam Van Culin who retires at the end of 1994 after more than a decade as Secretary General.

SOUTHERN AFRICA

The Meeting:
- gave thanks for the independence of Namibia, the end of civil war in Mozambique, and the announcement of elections in Lesotho;
- expressed hopes for the return of democracy in Swaziland;
- gave thanks for progress towards non-racial democracy in South Africa.

INTER-ANGLICAN BUDGET - CORE BUDGET
INCOME

AMENDED NOVEMBER 1992

	Past 1990 Actual £	Past 1991 Actual £	Current Triennium 1992 Budget £	Current Triennium 1992 Est'd Outturn £	Current Triennium 1993 Original Budget £	Current Triennium 1993 Est'd Outturn £	Notes	Next Triennium 1994 Draft Budget £	Next Triennium 1995 Draft Budget £	Next Triennium 1996 Draft Budget £
Interest on deposits	46.32	438.00	515,000	32,500	15,000	20,000		5,000	10,000	14,000
Publications sold	8,800	16,167	12,000	17,000	13,000	13,000		13,500	13,750	14,000
Services rendered to other bodies	10,260	10,583	9,000	6,500	3,000	500	P.E.F. cont	500	550	550
Rent Receivable	2,295	-	4,000	3,000	4,000	10,500		10,750	11,000	11,300
Grants for equipment	2,500	6,238	-	2,500	-	2,000		2,000	2,000	-
Contribution to relocation costs	10,000	10,000	5,000	2,800	-	-		-	-	-
	80,179	80,993	45,000	64,300	35,000	46,000		31,750	37,300	39,850
Grants & Special Contributions - for: Primates' Meeting	-	20,482	-	-	-	-		-	-	-
Mission & Evangelism Appt	-	16,000	-	-	?	-		-	-	-
Inter-Anglican Theological Consultation	-	22,915	-	-	-	-		-	-	-
Donations & Miscellaneous income	748	906	-	1,200	-	1,000		750	700	650
	80,927	141,296	45,000	65,500	35,000	47,000		32,500	38,000	40,500
Core budget contributions (Includes contributions recovered from previous years)	688,159	740,992	963,880	785,900	1,054,475	875,000		917,500	962,000	1,009,500
TOTAL INCOME	£769,086	£882,288	£1,008,880	£851,400	£1,089,475	£922,000		£950,000	£1,000,000	£1,050,000
								4.85%	4.85%	4.94%

187

INTER-ANGLICAN BUDGET - CORE BUDGET - CENTRAL SECRETARIAT

REVISED NOVEMBER 1992

EXPENDITURE

	Past 1990 Actual £	1991 Actual £	1992 Budget £	Current Triennium 1992 Est'd Outturn £	1993 Original Budget £	1993 Est'd Outturn £	Notes	Next Triennium 1994 Draft Budget £	1995 Draft Budget £	1996 Draft Budget £
Secretary General's Office										
Employment costs	100,905	113,425	115,000	122,000	135,000	135,000	NB Tfr of staff from Admin	156,000	145,000	156,000
Recruitment/relocation costs	-	-	8,000	-	5,000	5,000		10,000	-	-
Hospitality	1,998	2,220	2,700	1,500	2,900	2,000		2,500	2,500	2,500
Travel	6,660	4,668	7,000	5,500	7,500	7,500		8,000	8,250	8,500
Housing	5,698	7,127	6,500	4,500	7,000	7,000		7,500	6,500	6,750
Other costs including Quest	-	536	-	650	-	500		400	500	600
	115,261	127,976	139,200	134,150	157,400	157,000		184,400	162,750	174,350
Communication										
Employment costs	65,720	72,819	93,000	71,000	102,500	62,000		66,650	71,650	77,000
Hospitality	290	113	300	250	350	350		225	235	250
Travel	1,450	1,513	4,300	2,500	4,650	2,500		3,000	3,000	3,500
Publications	20,865	36,494	30,000	31,000	32,350	32,350		34,000	35,500	37,500
Books and Journals	1,587	1,610	1,750	1,500	1,875	1,875		1,950	2,050	2,125
Translation	-	-	5,375	-	5,775	5,775		2,625	2,750	2,900
Other costs including Quest	222	3,254	-	2,500	-	2,500		2,750	2,900	3,000
	90,134	115,803	134,725	108,750	147,500	107,350		111,200	118,085	126,275
Mission and Evangelism										
Employment costs	20,160	40,800	59,000	56,500	64,500	62,000		66,650	71,650	77,000
Hospitality	14	10	300	100	350	35		225	235	250
Travel	4,374	3,420	6,000	3,000	6,675	4,000		5,500	5,750	6,000
Decade of Evangelism - Publications	9,398	5,574	4,000	6,300	6,000	6,000		6,300	6,600	7,000
Other Costs				1,000						
	33,946	49,804	69,300	66,900	77,525	72,350		78,675	84,235	90,250
Liturgical Co-ordinator support	162	257	6,000	1,500	6,500	6,500		6,600	6,950	7,300
c/f	239,503	293,840	349,225	311,300	388,925	343,200		380,875	372,020	398,175

EXPENDITURE

	Past 1990 Actual £	1991 Actual £	1992 Budget £	Current Triennium 1992 Est'd Outturn £	1993 Original Budget £	1993 Est'd Outturn £	Notes	Next Triennium 1994 Draft Budget £	1995 Draft Budget £	1996 Draft Budget £
b/f	239,503	293,840	349,225	311,300	388,925	343,200		380,875	372,020	398,175
Ecumenical Relations										
Employment costs	49,171	63,370	64,000	59,000	70,500	53,000		45,000	48,000	51,600
Hospitality	212	115	300	350	350	350		225	235	250
Travel	2,315	4,817	4,300	3,000	4,650	3,000		4,900	5,125	5,400
Other costs including Quest	-	221	-	100	-	500		450	475	500
	51,698	68,523	68,600	62,450	75,500	56,850		50,575	53,835	57,750
Administration										
Employment costs	80,618	84,760	102,250	80,000	112,500	89,000		95,500	102,000	110,000
Travel	2,004	1,184	3,500	1,000	3,725	1,000		1,500	1,650	1,750
Office expenses	33,747	34,829	38,750	22,000	41,600	24,000		26,500	29,000	32,000
	116,369	120,773	144,500	103,000	157,825	114,00		123,500	132,650	143,750
Audit & other professional fees	9,517	12,900	8,800	12,250	9,600	9,600		8,500	9,000	9,500
Office rent and maintenance	64,343	67,256	81,000	71,750	82,000	74,000		77,000	79,000	81,000
Depreciation - I.T. equipment	15,930	9,714	12,500	) 9,500	12,500	10,200		10,200	10,200	10,200
Office furniture & equipment	10,000	11,246	-	) 3,300		3,300		3,300	3,300	3,300
Contribution to President's staff	750	825	900	900	1,000	950		1,000	1,050	1,100
Contingency Provision	-	-	14,000	-	11,500	-		32,500	35,000	40,000
Loss on exchange	13,769	-	-	-	-	-				
	114,309	101,941	117,200	97,700	116,600	98,050		132,500	137,550	145,100
Less transfer from Reserves	-	(4,750)	-	(4,750)	-	(4,750)		(4,750)	-	-
carried forward	521,879	580,327	679,525	569,700	738,850	607,350		682,700	696,055	744,775

INTER-ANGLICAN BUDGET - CORE BUDGET - SUMMARY

REVISED NOVEMBER 1992

EXPENDITURE	Past 1990 Actual £	1991 Actual £	1992 Budget £	Current Triennium 1992 Est'd Outturn £	1993 Original Budget £	1993 Est'd Outturn £	Notes	Next Triennium 1994 Draft Budget £	1995 Draft Budget £	1996 Draft Budget £
Central Secretariat Expenses b/f	521,879	580,327	679,525	569,700	738,850	607,350		682,700	696,055	744,775
Inter-Anglican responsibilities:										
Grant to Anglican Centre in Rome	48,158	40,871	40,000	37,500	42,250	37,750	Resolution 31	?	?	?
Provisions for Meetings, etc -										
Inter-Church Conversations	44,500	28,000	40,000	25,000	50,000	40,000	Res.31 (for 1992)	40,000	40,000	40,00
Mission Issues Advisory Group	20,000	7,500	8,000	8,000	10,000	10,000	"Missio" from 1994	10,000	12,000	12,000
Decade of Evangelism Consultation	-	-	12,000	-	12,000	-		-	-	-
Inter-Anglican Theological Con.	12,000	22,915	13,500	-	14,000	-	Res.31 (for 1992)	-	-	-
Meetings of the Council and Standing Committee	60,000	60,000	60,000	60,000	60,000	60,000		60,000	60,000	60,000
Primates' Meetings	8,000	65,482	30,000	30,000	30,000	30,000		40,000	45,000	50,000
Lambeth Conference	44,517	85,000	110,000	110,000	115,000	90,000		100,000	110,000	120,000
Research	1,650	1,800	2,000	2,000	2,200	2,200		2,200	2,300	2,500
TOTAL EXPENDITURE	760,704	891,895	995,025	842,200	1,074,300	877,300		934,900	965,355	1,029,275
Less INCOME	769,086	882,288	1,008,880	851,400	1,089,475	922,000		950,000	1,000,000	1,050,000
SURPLUS to restore General Reserve			£13,855	£9,200	£15,175	£44,700		£15,100	£34,645	£20,725
DEFICIT	£8,382	£9,607								

INTER-ANGLICAN BUDGET
PROPOSED REVISED PERCENTAGE CONTRIBUTIONS

	Proposed %	Revised changes %	
Australia	10.50	-	10.50
Brazil	0.50	-	0.50
(Burundi (			0.06
B R Z (Rwanda (	0.20	-0.02	0.06
(Zaire (			0.06
Canada	11.00	-	11.00
Central Africa	1.25	-	1.25
Ceylon	0.10	-	0.10
CCEA	1.00	-	1.00
England (incl. Diocese in Europe)	28.15	-	28.15
Indian Ocean	0.25	-	0.25
Ireland	2.25	-	2.25
Japan	1.25	-	1.25
Jerusalem & Middle East	0.50	-0.15	0.35
Kenya	1.50	-	1.50
Melanesia	0.10	-	0.10
Myanmar (Burma)	0.10	-	0.10
New Zealand	3.00	-	3.00
Nigeria	1.50	-	1.50
Papua New Guinea	0.10	-	0.10
Philippines	0.50	-	0.50
Scotland	1.50	-	1.50
Southern Africa	2.00	-0.25	1.75
Southern Cone of S America	0.25	-	0.25
Sudan	0.25	-	0.25
Tanzania	0.75	-0.25	0.50
Uganda	1.00	-0.25	0.75
USA	27.25	-	27.25
Wales	2.25	-	2.25
West Africa	0.35	-	0.35
West Indies	1.50	-0.50	1.00
United Churches			
Bangladesh	0.06	-0.01	0.05
Church of North India	0.10	-	0.10
Church of Pakistan	0.10	-	0.10
Church of South India	0.15	-	0.15
Extra-provincial Dioceses			
Bermuda	0.10	-	0.10
Lusitanian Church 0.05	-0.015	0.035	
Spanish Reformed Episcopal Church 0.05	-0.015	0.035	
	101.46	-1.46	100.00%

Effective - 1 January 1994

ANGLICAN CONSULTATIVE COUNCIL
Register of Participants for Cape Town 1993

OFFICERS:
President:
   The Most Revd and Rt Hon George L. Carey
   Archbishop of Canterbury
Chairman:
   The Revd Canon Colin Craston (England)
Vice Chairman:
   The Rt Revd Simon Chiwanga (Tanzania)
Secretary-General:
   The Revd Canon Samuel Van Culin
Standing Committee:
The Most Revd George Browne * ....(West Africa)
Mr Edgar Bradley...........................(Aotearoa, New Zealand and Polynesia)
Mrs Pamela Chinnis..(USA)
Mrs Betty Govinden...(Southern Africa)
The Most Revd Douglas Hambidge ....(Canada)
The Rt Revd Joseph Iida..(Japan)
The Rt Revd Alexander Malik * ....(Pakistan)

MEMBERS:
The Anglican Church in Aotearoa, New Zealand and Polynesia
   The Revd John Paterson
   Mr Edgar Bradley
The Anglican Church of Australia
   The Rt Revd Philip Newell
   The Very Revd David Richardson
   Dr Muriel Porter §
The Church of Bangladesh
   The Revd Birbal Haldar
The Episcopal Anglican Church of Brazil
   The Rt Revd Sumio Takatsu
The Church of the Province of Burundi
   The Revd Bernard Ntahoturi §

Appendices

The Anglican Church of Canada
 The Most Revd Douglas Hambidge
 The Revd Barbara Clay
 Dr Diane Maybee §
The Church of the Province of Central Africa
 The Rt Revd Bernard Malango
 Mr Michael Kututwa
The Church of Ceylon (Sri Lanka)
 The Rt Revd Andrew Kumarage
The Council of the Churches of East Asia
 The Most Revd Moses Tay
 Mr Tutik Garuda §
The Church of England
 The Rt Revd Colin James
 The Revd John Broadhurst
 Dr Christina Baxter
The Church of the Province of the Indian Ocean
 The Revd Roger Chung Po Chuen §
The Church of Ireland
 The Ven Michael Mayes
 Brenda Shiel
The Holy Catholic Church in Japan
 The Rt Revd Joseph Iida
The Episcopal Church in Jerusalem and the Middle East
 The Rt Revd John Brown
The Church of the Province of Kenya
 The Rt Revd David Gitari
 Mr Samuel Arap Ng'eny
The Anglican Church of Korea (became a Province April 1993)
The Church of the Province of Melanesia
 The Rt Revd James Mason
The Church of the Province of Myanmar (Burma)
 The Rt Revd Samuel Si Htay *
  Represented by the Revd Canon Monty Morris
The Church of the Province of Nigeria
 The Rt Revd Maxwell Anikwenwa
 The Very Revd Vincent Muoghereh
 The Hon Justice Christian Abimbola
The Church of North India
 The Most Revd John Ghose *
 The Revd Noel Sen

Membership

The Church of Pakistan
   The Rt Revd Alexander Malik *‡
   Mr Theodore Phailbus
The Anglican Church of Papua New Guinea
   The Rt Revd Tevita Talanoa *
The Philippine Episcopal Church
   The Most Revd Richard Abellon
The Province of the Episcopal Church of Rwanda
   The Rt Revd Jonathan Ruhumuliza
   The Revd Athanase Ngirinshuti
   Mrs Lydia Nyiramugisha
The Scottish Episcopal Church
   The Very Revd Ian Watt *
   Represented by Mr John Rea
The Church of the Province of Southern Africa
   The Rt Revd Dinis Sengulane
   The Revd Canon Malusi Mpumlwana
   Mrs Betty Govinden
The Anglican Church of the Southern Cone of America
   The Revd Julio Bustos
The Church of South India
   The Rt Revd David Pothirajulu
   The Revd Peter Sugandhar
   Prof Samuel Kadakaseril *
   Represented by Prof George Koshy
The Episcopal Church of the Sudan
   The Rt Revd Michael Lugor *
   Represented by the Revd Eluzai Mogga Ladu
   The Revd Nelson Nyombe
The Church of the Province of Tanzania
   The Rt Revd Charles Mwaigoga
   The Revd Mkunga Mtingele
The Church of the Province of Uganda
   The Most Revd Yona Okoth
   The Revd Canon Wilson Baganizi
   Mr Edward Mungati
The Episcopal Church of the United States of America
   The Rt Revd Mark Dyer
   The Revd Austin Cooper, Jr
   Mrs Pamela Chinnis

Appendices

The Church in Wales
 The Most Revd Alwyn Rice Jones
 The Revd Canon David Williams
The Church of the Province of West Africa
 The Most Revd George Browne *
 Represented by the Rt Revd Joseph Dadson
The Church in the Province of the West Indies
 The Rt Revd Clive Abdulah
 The Ven Alvin Stone
The Province of the Anglican Church of Zaire
 The Rt Revd Tibafa Mugera

* indicates not in attendance Cape Town 1993
§ newly elected Standing Committee (ACC)
‡ continues on Standing Committee (ACC)

THE PRIMATES OF THE ANGLICAN COMMUNION

The Most Revd and Rt Hon George Carey
 Primus inter pares – England
The Most Revd Brian Davis
 Aotearoa, New Zealand and Polynesia
The Most Revd Keith Rayner
 Australia
The Most Revd Barnabas Mondal
 Bangladesh
The Most Revd Olavo Luiz
 Brazil
The Most Revd Samuel Sindamuka
 Burundi
The Most Revd Michael Peers
 Canada
The Most Revd Khotso Makhulu
 Central Africa
The Most Revd Moses Tay
 East Asia
The Most Revd French Chang-Him
 Indian Ocean

The Most Revd Robert Eames
    Ireland
The Most Revd Christopher Kikawada
    Japan
The Most Revd Samir Kafity
    Jerusalem and the Middle East
The Most Revd Manasses Kuria
    Kenya
The Most Revd Amos Waiaru
    Melanesia
The Most Revd Andrew Mya Han
    Myanmar
The Most Revd Joseph Adetiloye*
    Nigeria
The Most Revd John Ghose *
    North India
The Most Revd Zahir ud din Mirza
    Pakistan
The Most Revd Bevan Meredith
    Papua New Guinea
The Most Revd Richard Abellon
    Philippines
The Most Revd Augustin Nshamihigo
    Rwanda
The Most Revd Richard Holloway
    Scotland
The Most Revd Desmond Tutu
    Southern Africa
The Most Revd Colin Bazley
    Southern Cone
The Most Revd Vasant Dandin
    South India
The Most Revd Benjamina Yugusuk
    Sudan
The Most Revd John Ramadhani
    Tanzania
The Most Revd Yona Okoth
    Uganda
The Most Revd Edmond Browning
    USA
The Most Revd Alwyn Rice Jones
    Wales

Appendices

The Most Revd George Browne *
   West Africa
   Represented by The Rt Revd Joseph Dadson
The Most Revd Orland Lindsay
   West Indies
The Most Revd Byankya Njojo
   Zaire

* indicates not in attendance Cape Town 1993

On 6 January, Epiphany, the Most Revd Narciso Ticobay was enthroned Prime Bishop of the Philippine Episcopal Church

The Primates of England, West Indies, Ireland, Indian Ocean, Aotearoa, New Zealand and Polynesia and Jerusalem and the Middle East form the Standing Committee for the Primates.

The Primate of Canada chairs the Inter-Anglican Finance Committee from 1993.

REQUIESCANT IN PACE

The Most Revd George Browne, Primate of West Africa
Died 14 February 1993

The Most Revd Olavo Luiz, Primate of Brazil
Died 8 March 1993

May they rest in peace and rise in glory

✠

CO-OPTED MEMBERS
Mrs Ruth Yangsoon Choi ....(Korea)
Mr Cesar Guzman..(Southern Cone)
Mr Tim Goodes...(Australia)
Mrs Faga T Matalavea ....(Aotearoa, New Zealand, Polynesia)
The Rt Revd James Ottley ....(USA/Panama)
The Rt Revd Fernando Soares ....(Lusitanian Church of Portugal)

PARTICIPANTS FROM OTHER CHURCHES
The Rt Revd Dr Joseph Mar Irenaeus..........................(Mar Thoma Church)
The Most Revd Antonius Glazemaker.......................(Old Catholic Church)
The Revd Dr Milton Efthimiou ....(Greek Orthodox Church)
Monsignor Kevin McDonald................................(Roman Catholic Church)
Bishop William Oden...(Methodist Church)
The Revd Dr Frank Chikane...............(South African Council of Churches)
The Revd Dr Eugene Brand.............................(Lutheran World Federation)

CONSULTANTS/SPEAKERS
The Rt Revd Michael Nazir-Ali..........Church Missionary Society, England
The Revd John Pobee ....World Council of Churches, Switzerland

PRIMATES' PERSONAL STAFF
The Revd Canon Roger Symon ....(England)
The Revd Gordon Light ....(Canada)
The Revd Patrick Mauney ....(USA)
The Revd Canon John Lathrop..(For Uganda)
The Revd Eluzai Mogga ....(Sudan)

CHAIR – INTER-ANGLICAN FINANCE COMMITTEE
The Rt Revd Edward Luscombe ....(Scotland)

STAFF
The Revd Donald Anderson......................Secretary for Ecumenical Affairs
Mrs Christine Codner
Mrs Elizabeth Coy
Miss Clare Dell...Lambeth Palace
The Revd Paul Gibson ....Liturgical Officer
Mrs Denise Line
Mrs Deirdre Martin
Mr John Martin..Church of England Newspaper
The Revd Cyril Okorocha.................Secretary for Mission and Evangelism

Appendices

The Rt Revd Sir Paul Reeves........Anglican Observer at the United Nations
The Rt Revd Paul Richardson ....Papua New Guinea
Mr James Rosenthal ....Secretary for Communication
The Revd Michael Sams..............Secretary for Finance and Administration
Ms Vanessa Wilde

SECONDED INTERNATIONAL COMMUNICATIONS TEAM
Mr John Allen ....(Southern Africa)
The Revd Patrick Forbes...(England)
Ms Sonia Francis ....(USA)
Mrs Liz Gibson Harries..(Ireland)
The Revd Dr Charles and Mrs Nancy Long.......................................(USA)
Ms Estelle Marinus ....(Southern Africa)
The Ven. Lynn Ross ....(Canada)
Mr Jim Thrall...(USA)
Mr Doug Tindal..(Canada)

HOST PROVINCE STAFF CO-ORDINATORS
The Revd Ronald Jonathan
The Revd Rowan Smith
The Rt Revd Winston Ndungane
The Rt Revd Michael Nuttall
Mr George Gibbs

INTER-ANGLICAN INFORMATION NETWORK STAFF
Mr Clifford Hicks ....(Australia)
The Revd Clement Lee ....(USA)
Mr Stewart Ting Chong ....(Southern Africa)

VIDEO TEAM
The Revd Robert Browne ....(ACO/USA)
Mr Todd FitzGerald
Mr Andrew Stauffer ....(USA)

TRAVEL AGENT
Mr Ajay Sodha

Membership

THE MEMBER CHURCHES OF THE ANGLICAN COMMUNION

The Anglican Church in Aotearoa, New Zealand and Polynesia
The Anglican Church of Australia
The Episcopal Anglican Church of Brazil
The Church of the Province of Burundi
The Anglican Church of Canada
The Church of the Province of Central Africa
The Church of Ceylon (Sri Lanka) *Extra Provincial*
The Council of the Churches of East Asia
The Church of England
The Church of the Province of the Indian Ocean
The Church of Ireland
The Holy Catholic Church in Japan
The Episcopal Church in Jerusalem and the Middle East
The Church of the Province of Kenya
The Anglican Church of Korea (became a Province April 1993)
The Church of the Province of Melanesia
The Church of the Province of Myanmar (Burma)
The Church of the Province of Nigeria
The Anglican Church of Papua New Guinea
The Philippine Episcopal Church
The Province of the Episcopal Church of Rwanda
The Scottish Episcopal Church
The Church of the Province of Southern Africa
The Anglican Church of the Southern Cone of America
The Episcopal Church of the Sudan
The Church of the Province of Tanzania
The Church of the Province of Uganda
The Episcopal Church of the United States of America
The Church in Wales
The Church of the Province of West Africa
The Church in the Province of the West Indies
The Province of the Anglican Church of Zaire

THE UNITED CHURCHES – IN FULL COMMUNION

The Church of South India
The Church of North India
The Church of Pakistan
The Church of Bangladesh

Appendices

EXTRA PROVINCIAL CHURCHES – IN FULL COMMUNION

The Lusitanian Church of Portugal
The Spanish Reformed Episcopal Church